ECCENTRIC MINISTRY

ECCENTRIC MINISTRY

PASTORAL CARE AND LEADERSHIP IN THE PARISH

Christopher Moody

Foreword by Richard Harries

Darton, Longman and Todd
London

First published in 1992 by
Darton, Longman and Todd Ltd
89 Lillie Road, London SW6 1UD

ISBN 0–232–51978–1

A catalogue record for this book is available
from the British Library

Cover: *Cornfield by Moonlight, with Evening Star,*
c. 1830 by Samuel Palmer (detail);
reproduced by courtesy of the British Museum.
Design by Judy Linard

Phototypeset by Intype, London
Printed and bound in Great Britain
at the University Press, Cambridge

CONTENTS

To Gill, Mike, Ann
Leslie, Richard, Ivor
and all my other friends and teachers

FOREWORD

THIS IS PASTORAL theology at its very best. Christopher Moody faces fully and honestly many of the feelings which trouble priests and ministers today. He is sensitive to the lack of clarity and certainty about our role, the conflicting voices and sources of authority in society, the confused expectations and the lack of valuation by many. What distinguishes this book from others, however, is that he uses these feelings and this unsettling situation to recover a deeper and more biblical understanding of what it is to be a pastor today. He is therefore critical of many of the ways in which clergy have tried to reassure themselves by adopting an alien role model, that of the professional from the nineteenth century, and that of the counsellor or community worker from the twentieth century. He argues instead that there is something inherently uncertain, in the world's terms, about our role and *raison d'être*, which has to do with the very nature of our mission.

The book is also particularly helpful for the way the author rejects many of the current polarities, for example that between pastoral work and evangelism. He argues that in the modern world pastoral work, properly understood, is inevitably evangelistic, not in the sense that people are being coerced to believe but because pastoral work is a sharing in the mission of God. It is an initiative, a moving out into the world which God cherishes, in which Christ is present and which he is seeking to bring to fulfilment. In order to minister to this world at all, and this is a task shared by priest and people, it is necessary to enter into that mixture of half belief and no belief that characterizes it. This inevitably means trying to communicate the gospel in terms which such people can understand.

As Vicar of Fulham (All Saints), where Christopher served a four-year title, I was able to witness at first hand his sensitive, caring and thoughtful ministry, his gift with both young and old and his refusal to accept quick or easy solutions. After a period ministering in Surbiton, he became Chaplain of King's College, London, when I was Dean. Student chaplaincy is a particularly difficult form of ministry and it was this which helped Christopher to reflect on why his instinctively Christian attitudes led him to refuse to be pressed into the mould of a counsellor or professional. It was in the fleeting exchanges with students in the corridor, chats in the bar or lingering after chapel that he not only discovered but was able to affirm fully a Christian ministry that was every bit as valid, in its own terms, as those which like to have everything buttoned up and under control. After King's he went to minister in a very mixed inner city parish which again has provided much valuable experience for the reflection which emerges in this book. He is a naturally perceptive person, whose sharp intelligence and instincts have been honed by studies in history, sociology and psychology and by novelists, as well as by theology and spirituality.

I believe that this is a book which will prove enormously helpful to a great many exercising a pastoral ministry today. Reading it gives one a new sense of confidence and faith, even excitement, even amidst the uncertainty, confusion and lack of validation. For it is above all a book rooted in faith and trust in what God is doing through his people today.

RICHARD HARRIES
BISHOP OF OXFORD

INTRODUCTION

L ET ME BEGIN with two personal anecdotes.

PASSING THE MONUMENT

Lambeth Cemetery is about four miles distance from my parish and to get there I usually ask for a lift from the undertaker. As we drive into the cemetery through the gates, the first thing that greets me is a family monument in black marble belonging to one of the local undertakers. I always use it as a visual reminder that the business of death is as much his preserve as mine. Many families will have had an association with the same undertakers which has lasted several generations. To these families the cemetery chapel is as much a church as a parish church would be, and I am a religious functionary employed for a particular purpose. Rather, I imagine, like a Shinto priest in Japan, I am a representative of an official religion which the family may not actually adhere to, but whose presence ensures that things are done properly.

Mentally I make a little bow to the monument as we pass because it is a reminder to me that I am not on my own territory. Any space for religion is a matter of negotiation between me, the undertaker, and the bereaved. I am constrained by many factors, such as the time allotted for the service, the music, and the stage management, over which I have little or no control. But I am conscious that this is the environment in which I have been asked to make my contribution, and I must therefore make the best of it.

For me, the undertaker's monument has become a symbol

of the Church's position in modern society. In former times the Church enjoyed a virtual monopoly, especially in matters like death, both of the content of belief and of the way it was communicated – the medium *and* the message. Now, however, those of us identified in various ways as ministers of the Church often work in a pastoral environment in which there are many other voices with authority as well as our own. It is impossible to predict beforehand, from one group of people to another, what will be the content of their belief and what form and expression they will give to it. Until relatively recently it was still possible, because of the status afforded to churches and their ministers, for clergy to behave as if no other voices existed; but anyone working outside the confines of a church congregation (or even *within* it!) today, recognizes that that situation has changed. We cannot assume to know what exists in a particular pastoral context before we enter it. We are forced to realize that the territory we enter is not ours alone. We cannot be sure of the impact that our own communication is going to have within the conversation between different authorities which began before we entered the field and will continue long after we have left again – including many voices we may not even be conscious of ourselves.

This leads to two conclusions which form the basis of the discussion of pastoral activity in this book. First, it is impossible to distinguish too closely between pastoral activity on one hand, and missionary or evangelistic activity on the other. This is not because nowadays ministers are forced to use pastoral situations as an opportunity for evangelism, but because to create the space to enable communication on a pastoral level to take place involves an acknowledgement of the presence of a variety of belief and unbelief among all the participants. The more clearly this context is mapped out, the more space will be created for real pastoral contact. This mapping never stops, because every pastoral encounter is at the same time a missionary journey from our own known world into unknown, or only half-known, territory.

Secondly, what characterizes a lot of pastoral encounters today is that they are often transitory. Nobody is completely in control of what takes place. Even the undertaker is not exempt. The undertaker's monument may proclaim his long association with the cemetery, but the borough runs it. He may call himself 'funeral director' – i.e. the person in control – but as his older title implies, he is still there, primarily, to undertake the wishes of the deceased and the bereaved. In modern pastoral situations there is often no single source of authority, and it is difficult to discern what or whom is most to be trusted or believed. Mass communication influences and shapes our lives in a profound way, making us more like each other on one level, but at the same time introducing each of us to many more voices and authorities than we previously knew existed.

It is very difficult in such situations to know precisely what measure of authority we, as ministers, have been given, and this leads to a lot of confusion about what expectations of the minister's role are actually present in any encounter. We are often made aware simultaneously that there is a level of need or concern asking for some sort of response, but at the same time that our ministrations may be rejected as inadequate or irrelevant. This dual awareness is well brought out in R. S. Thomas' poem 'The Priest'.

> The priest picks his way
> Through the parish. Eyes watch him
> From windows, from the farms;
> Hearts wanting him to come near.
> The flesh rejects him.[1]

This is a very uncomfortable level of awareness to sustain, and it leads us, either to emphasize those aspects of our role over which we have most power of self-projection and definition, or alternatively to concentrate on developing levels of professional expertise which we feel may be more generally accepted. This means in practice that those sorts of encounter which are by their nature fleeting and obscure are undervalued and neglected in favour of those over which we have most control. This in turn restricts pastoral activity to a narrower and narrower field in a society where more and more contacts are of a transitory nature.

The aim of this book is to ask what might be gained by

trying to work in the full knowledge that we are *not* entirely in control, either of the situations to which we are introduced, or of what we are held to represent by the other participants. What other presences and sources of understanding and healing are evoked by the presence of someone who is understood to be there, in some sense, on God's behalf? This leads on to my second anecdote.

A CHAPLAIN'S DILEMMA

Before I became a vicar, I was a chaplain in a large city college. There had been a chaplain in the college ever since it had been founded – over 150 years ago – and traditionally he had been responsible for the pastoral care of the students. This task was still vaguely assumed by the academic staff to constitute most of what the chaplain had to do, though the use they made of me as a person to whom students with problems could be referred was haphazard. No such assumption, however, was made by the majority of the students, many of whom had no expectations of me at all. Most of my pastoral work among them was carried out as a result of my own initiatives, with individuals and various student societies and groups.

The scope for establishing a stable pastoral relationship with all but a few students in a very fluid institution, which virtually doubled in size while I was there, and in which the pressures on time were considerable, was limited. It was obvious that I would have to change my approach to the pastoral task if I was to survive without accumulating a burden of guilt, caught between what was expected, traditionally, by the institution and what was actually possible. For the first time I became aware of quite how contradictory many expectations of the pastoral task were, including my own.

At the same time the college began to develop a proper structure of student services, including an accommodation office and a medical centre with two full-time and one part-time psychotherapists, and a psychiatrist. The question began to present itself, how should we, as professionally trained individuals charged by the institution with the welfare of students, relate to each other? This question became acute when the suggestion was made that the job of chaplain and part-time student counsellor might be combined. I was convinced that, though the results in terms of an increase in the general well-being of individuals might look the same, the assumptions and methods of working which lay behind pastoral care on the one hand and psychotherapeutic counselling on the other were sufficiently different to make it difficult for one individual to combine the two roles within the same institution. In particular it seemed to me that there would be a conflict between an active ministry which, as I understood it, made use of common memories and expectations of moral and spiritual authority and mediated it in the care of individuals, and the more passive role of the psychotherapist in allowing a person to find their own solutions by re-enacting their own relationship with significant others, using transference and projection. Moreover, I realized that counselling of this sort is very time-consuming and would have seriously undermined any attempts to pursue a wider role than the care of individuals.

I began to ask myself how this confusion could have arisen in the minds of the powers-that-be in the college, and how far it mirrored my own confusion about what was at the root of the pastoral task. Was the basis for my effectiveness as a pastor my own training and expertise as a professional working alongside other professionals? Or did it draw upon much deeper sources of shared belief and theological understanding? What was most important? My own sense of professionalism? Or on the other hand, common expectations of God's gracious activity? Could this gracious activity be represented in the evangelism and pastoral care undertaken not only by a professional élite but in the action of the whole people of God? What rearrangement of pastoral priorities might be needed if one thought of the primary motive for the pastoral task as the proclamation or disclosure of God's kingdom, rather than the care of individuals within existing communities of whatever kind?

In the course of thinking things through I did indeed come to feel that my understanding of the pastoral task had become too detached from its roots in the belief that God is dynamically at work, immanently and redemptively, in his own creation, towards a final fulfilment. It is our privilege as pastors, co-workers and people of God, to discern this activity in whatever situation to which we are called and, in some way, to release and embody it in our own lives. To return to these roots means, I believe, to discard many of the notions about professional pastoral ministry which have helped to imprison this activity within church congregations, and to reach back to a different understanding of it as something authenticated on the basis of shared faith rather than claims to a particular professional competence and status.

1

MODELS FOR MINISTRY

IF PASTORAL CARE is more a matter of shared belief than professional competence, what beliefs about God underlie the pastoral task, and what models for pastoral ministry and leadership do they give rise to?

Most of us work to more than one model, depending on what pastoral situation we are involved in, whether it is, for example, pastoral care within a congregation or some form of outreach work in our local area. But, for the sake of clarity, let us divide these models into two sorts: the incarnational or sacramental, and the redemptive.

THE INCARNATIONAL AND SACRAMENTAL MODEL

God is present, potentially at least, in all that he has created and in all people who are made in his image. The Church and its worship is the sign and sacrament of God's presence in the world but his presence is not confined to the Church. The Church fulfils its nature as the sacrament of God's presence by pointing to his presence and celebrating it in all its human manifestations, individual and corporate. There are two ways of apprehending this presence: the open and revealed way of public worship and the hidden way of pastoral ministry and intercession. The images of Christ which often most motivate pastoral activity in this model are that of the Christ of Nazareth – the helpless baby or the hidden Christ; and the suffering Christ of the cross – the victim.

This model has inspired some of the best examples of Christian service. In our own day, one thinks especially of the hospice movement and the work inspired by Mother Teresa of Calcutta. The daily prayer of Mother Teresa begins:

> Dearest Lord, may I see you today and every day in the person of the sick, and whilst nursing them minister unto you. Though you hide yourself behind the unattractive disguise of the irritable, the exacting, the unreasonable, may I still recognize you and say: 'Jesus, my patient, how sweet it is to serve you.'[1]

The heart of such work is identification with the hidden Christ who is already present. The work needs no further justification. The work we know about, like Mother Teresa's, is itself a sign, a sacrament, pointing to the presence of God in a myriad unknown acts in response to human need, among believers and non-believers alike.

The work of a Mother Teresa is one of the greatest contemporary witnesses to the Christian gospel, undertaken as the result of a special call and gift from God. But how does the model work for those of us without such a special call, working in parishes as part of the ordained ministry? Here, I think, we can see dangers.

First, it does not help us to order our pastoral priorities, except by tilting them in the direction of response to human need. We cannot do everything. How do we give priority to one call for help over another, given that they are both manifestations of Christ's hidden presence in human suffering? Perhaps the question betrays a need to keep control, when, as Mother Teresa's own life shows, great things happen when we lose control (she was already doing a good job within a teaching order when she received the call to care for the dying). On the other hand, the feeling of being pulled in too many directions at the same time is less of a help than a hindrance.

Secondly, the model encourages a sharp distinction between pastoral care and other aspects of the Church's mission, like evangelism. When someone says, 'I'm more of a pastor than evangelist,' we know exactly what they mean. Many Christians, lay and ordained, find themselves torn between the call to be responsive to human need, and therefore to identify with and get alongside others, and the call to evangelize others, which they see as an act of persuasion which is in some ways incompatible with such identification. (I shall argue elsewhere that the two activities are actually closer than they look.) Many aspects of pastoral care entail the underlying assumption of some kind of authority, spiritual or professional, whilst on the other hand, evangelism carried out without regard for pastoral priorities often becomes a form of spiritual tyranny. At this point it is sufficient to say that the model allows a split to occur between the hidden and suffering Christ known in pastoral encounters and the Risen Christ, the Lord of the Church, proclaimed in evangelism.

Thirdly, whilst the model acknowledges that God can be disclosed in many spheres of human life in which he is not directly named, it does not recognize the dynamic character of this presence. This is bound to be the case if God is pictured only as helpless victim or suffering love. It does not sufficiently take into account that, according to Jewish and Christian belief, creation itself is moving towards an end under the guiding providence of God. This leaves room for two contrary stances in regard to pastoral activity: one of inaction, where we simply 'baptize' and celebrate as the Church what other people and other institutions do; or one of intense engagement in various issues and problems alongside others, combined with an uncritical acceptance of their goals and objectives, professional or political. Chaplains working in the armed services, hospitals, industry and schools will have a particularly acute sense of what I mean.

THE REDEMPTIVE MODEL

The incarnational model is more likely to influence us the further we move away from the boundaries of church life. The redemptive model is likely to become prominent the more we think about pastoral care within and around church congregations, because it conveys a sense of the Church as the saved community, the locus and agent of God's presence.

Often, in this model, the world is perceived as an evil place. Human philosophies, institutions and individual lives all lie under divine judgement. Social life in general, and individual lives in particular, are so corrupted that they convey little or no sign of the presence of God, nor of humankind as made in his image. Thus, even the highest forms of human thought and action are potentially evil or misleading if they are not balanced or completed by an open acknowledgement of God's sovereignty. Referring back to Mother Teresa, I have heard her work criticized by some Christians for being unchristian, because it did not include the active proselytizing of the dying. What did comfort in their dying hours or minutes matter in comparison with their eternal destination, which, in these critics' opinion, depended on an open acknowledgement of Jesus Christ as their Lord and Saviour?

The differences from the previous model could not be put more starkly. There is no sense, in this criticism, that Christ may be met in the dying, that an act of care may be worthy in itself, nor of any claim to respect that the dying may have as those going through the same experience as Christ. Christ died and rose again in a once-for-all attempt to rescue fallen humanity. Now he can be met only as the proclaimed Christ, the Risen Christ of the Church.

Of course, such opinions are not usually expressed in such an extreme form. Nor do they preclude real pastoral involve-ment and concern. Many of the great attempts to ameliorate the social conditions of the urban poor in the nineteenth century were undertaken by people who were convinced that ignorance, poverty and vice endangered the victims' eternal souls. Social reformers motivated by such opinions were wil-ling to venture into situations which those with perhaps more liberal opinions or a more complacent faith were content to leave alone. Often their work of saving souls involved them in confrontation with powerful blocs of vested interest – the brewers, for example, in the case of the anti-drink crusades, or factory owners, in the case of those who worked for the reduction of factory hours and the observance of Sunday as a day of rest. But, as these examples show, where the redemp-tive model is strong, the expression of pastoral activity is likely to be one of conflict rather than identification. Engagement with the world beyond the believing community is seen more in terms of the unmasking of evils rather than the disclosure of what is good.

The redemptive model has great strengths. In particular it has a strong sense of the dynamic power of God, of the need for no other justification for pastoral action other than faith, and of working towards the fulfilment of a greater vision. But equally, these strengths are often the source of dangerous distortions.

First, there is a tendency to look on all types of pastoral activity either as a form of pre-evangelism, in the case of work among those outside the church, or as a means of maintaining conformity among the members within it. The value of pastoral activity itself as an expression of the nature of the Church and its mission is weakened by its subservience to the primary task of evangelism. A sermon as the price for a bed for the night, a prayer as the price for attention, is a phenomenon called in some parts of the world 'rice Christianity'. Usually it is not as crude as that; but pastoral work and attempts to establish pastoral contact are often undermined by the sense that they hide an ulterior motive.

Secondly, this approach leaves little room for hints and guesses. Pastoral work is undertaken as a result of what we know and what we can give, not of what we may find out or receive. Nor does this approach leave much room for genuine disagreement. If little or no status is given to the person to be helped and the answers they give to their situation, there is no room either for genuine dialogue. This in turn has the effect of undermining the genuineness of some forms of contact. How much room for real dialogue, for example, is allowed in the Christian counselling programmes offered by some churches, and how much for outright persuasion?

Thirdly, whereas the fault of the first model is often to ignore altogether the issue of authority in pastoral contact, in the redemptive model the authority given to pastoral leaders is often too great, and untested. Because there is little expectation of finding God at work in the world outside the community of the redeemed, and no value is given to voices other than those within that community, there is little to balance their power, which is often further enhanced by very authoritarian images and language about God himself. As a chaplain

I came across churches proselytizing among students, in which members were set to watch over each other in a system of pastoral supervision, sometimes referred to as 'heavy shepherding'. These churches made a deliberate attempt to cut off the recently converted from any source of support, advice and authority outside the church's own system of leadership. Most Christians would recognize this as a form of spiritual tyranny undermining the true nature of the Church as a pastoral community. But there is logic in the position once the saved community becomes identified as the only locus and agent of God's gracious activity.

It is important to be aware of what models are actually in operation in a particular context. If someone is asking for help on one level while the pastor is attempting to provide an answer at another, the pastor's intervention is unlikely to be regarded as helpful. Often there has to be some negotiation about the models before a real pastoral exchange can begin.

The two issues about which people working according to these two models disagree most frequently are the relationship between evangelism and pastoral ministry in the mission of the Church, and the issue of authority. This difference arises from deeper differences about how the presence of God is apprehended in the world and in the community of believers. Is there a way of bringing the two ways together in a model which recognizes that the Church is God's agent and instrument of redemption as well as the sacrament of his presence in the world, but which also recognizes that God cannot be contained by the Church, and that his activity is not defined only by its ministry? Is there room for a third model for ministry, one which may have a special relevance for modern conditions?

THE WILDERNESS MODEL

Carlo Carretto wrote a book called *The Desert in the City*[2] – a title which refers at once to the experience of the breakdown of traditional sources of community and identity in the urban wasteland, and also to the possibility of using these conditions to find God. What characterizes everyone's experience in the modern city, in which so many different social worlds and ways of living exist side by side in an ever-changing pattern – an experience also often marked by loneliness and uprootedness – is its fragmentary and fleeting nature. Our modern environment often seems inimical to the truly personal, and there are few stable points of reference which can be said to point, like sacraments, to the presence of God in and behind everything. On the other hand, in such an environment people may bind themselves to excessively authoritarian regimes, or make one aspect of their life, such as work or sex, a be-all and end-all, as the only way of providing a stable source of personal identity and purpose. Any model which seeks to preserve an attitude of openness to the world, whilst maintaining a sense of purpose which goes beyond it, must take these aspects of modern experience fully into account.

The wilderness model recognizes that the world is full of presences, some of them divine, some of them demonic. Our experience of living in such an environment is full of ambivalences. According to the wilderness model, God is still understood to be encountered 'out there' in the world, as well as within the company of the redeemed. To obey the call of God in evangelism and pastoral action is to go out with him into the wilderness.

But the wilderness, as we know from the biblical accounts of the testing of the people of Israel and of Jesus, is a place of conflict as well as disclosure. Therefore we cannot determine beforehand, when entering a situation, whether our attitude should be one of resistance or acceptance. The wilderness itself will give us no clear clues as to the direction in which we may find God. For this we must rely on what we already 'know' about God within the company of believers. However, God is always moving beyond what we already know about him, and when we meet him in the wilderness, the encounter will still have about it something of the unexpected. Thus, according to this understanding, the mission of the Church is a pilgrimage in which we grow in faith and knowledge as we continue in the way. The goal of evangelism and pastoral care alike is not to gather people in and keep them in one place, but to nurture them and keep them on the move.

In the wilderness, nothing is taken for granted and all

things are tested, including leadership. The wilderness is the place where human leadership is sought, but also broken. Moses grows in stature from the stammerer who meets God in the burning bush to the lawgiver at Sinai, but his failure nevertheless prevents him from entering the Promised Land. God is always in front of his people as an ultimate source of authority which cannot be entirely contained in their sacraments or leadership. This is Solomon's insight too when, at the point of his greatest achievement in the building of the Temple, he cries: 'But will God indeed dwell on the earth? Behold heaven and the highest heaven cannot contain thee; how much less the house which I have built' (1 Kings 8: 27 RSV).

Here we have an understanding of leadership in the Church which is based at root on what particular people in particular contexts help to disclose, rather than one based on the innate personal qualities, experience and professional status of the individual leader. All authority in the Church is, as it were, 'lent' by God. The Church itself only exists in that gap of time between the coming of Christ and the fulfilment of all things in him when all authority will be surrendered to God without the need of any intermediaries (cf. 1 Corinthians 15. 20–28). Thus spiritual authority hovers over particular people and particular functions, but it is not exclusive to them. They are foci, not containers, for an authority which God shares with his people as they obey his summons to come with him into the wilderness of the world.

I hope, in the following chapters, to unpack this very compressed statement in relation to the way ordained ministers see their work today, within church congregations and outside them. But I want to suggest at the outset, without seeking to replace the other two models entirely, the strengths which this wilderness model of ministry has in comparison with them.

First, it characterizes the world as disputed territory in which various powers and authorities are in operation. No one is entirely in control, including God who has willed it should be so. Nevertheless God's providential ordering of the world and our experience of it can be discovered in the act of faith which God himself enables, because he continues to call us in and through our experience of the world. This view of the world does full justice to the ambiguities and pitfalls we encounter in our experience, and to the need for judgement and discernment, without depriving us of the expectation that our ordinary experience can be sacramental, disclosing traces of the divine presence.

Secondly, it provides a balance between disclosure and conflict models for pastoral activity. This activity can be both a meeting of Christ in others *and* a liberation from hostile forces.

Thirdly, it does justice to both the active and passive dimensions of pastoral experience. It leaves us room for understanding it as a way of receiving what God is trying to reveal to us as well as for acting on God's behalf.

Finally, it preserves the eschatological perspective, the faith that everything is moving towards a final end. I have already hinted that the dangers associated with the other two models occur when this perspective is forgotten, either in an incarnational model which drives a wedge between the suffering Christ and the exalted One, or in a realized eschatology which sees membership of the saved community as in itself the goal for all mission and evangelism. God is bigger than the Church. The Church is possessed by him, not the other way round. In a real sense, we are not in control of ourselves or of our mission because God is. A defect shared by both the other models without this perspective is that they provide far too much control, either in the weight they give to our definitions of how God is present under the surface of ever-changing circumstances and experience, or in the authority with which we enter changing situations. On the analogy of the pillar of cloud (Exodus 13), we must understand that the presence of God, or at least our apprehension of it in our contemporary experience, is always dynamic and changing.

2

SHEPHERD OF ISRAEL

YEARS AGO, I saw a film by the Taviani brothers called *Padre, Padrone* – a title which is itself a play of words on the theme of authority, inadequately translated, *My father, my master*. The film is based on the autobiography of a Sardinian shepherd who became a writer. As a boy he was subject to the traditional, absolute control that a father could exert over his sons, which meant that at the age of about nine his father forcibly removed him from school and set him to look after the sheep in the summer pastures in the mountains.

There is a tremendous amount in the film which is relevant to our whole discussion in this book. It contrasts very vividly the world of tradition, communal identity, accepted status and enforced custom with the modern world of freedom, anonymity, the sense of being an individual and achieving personal goals. This becomes important when making comparisons between traditional forms of caring like 'pastoring' and modern forms of professional care. But it is its portrayal of the world of the hill shepherd, which assists us in the leap of imagination required in contemplating the biblical imagery about shepherding, which is my main reason for mentioning it at this point.

During the months when he is with the flock alone, the boy's identification with his sheep is total. Their world is his world. There is no superfluity and no means of escape. He lives with them, sleeps with them, uses their milk and occasionally slaughters one of them for meat and covering. He is subject to the same conditions and the same dangers as the flock. He must protect them. He will seriously affect the fortunes of his family if he loses any of them, and of course he is held accountable for them.

The boy is introduced to a world of intense loneliness, in which inward thoughts and imaginings sometimes assume a frightening importance. But it is also a place of vision. It is a world where long periods of boredom and inactivity are suddenly interrupted by great dangers or opportunities demanding all his resources of skill and decision. A world harsher in some ways than any prison regime, but, at the same time, of amazing freedom. Paradoxically, it is in this world to which he has been banished, that the boy in the film finds the inner resources to resist his father and escape his father's world altogether. At the end of the film, he is conscripted into the Italian army. He makes friends with other conscripts from all over Italy and learns to speak Italian rather than his local dialect, and to read and write. He returns home for a final showdown with his father, then leaves forever. The audience is left with a sense of triumph, but also of loss, as the boy leaves his former world, never to return.

The world he leaves behind is recognizably the same world as that of the nomadic shepherd in the Bible – people like the patriarchs, Moses and David. And something of the savour of that world, its sense of vision, accountability and loneliness still clings to priests, pastors and ministers even today. If the Shorter Oxford Dictionary gives as its first definition of the word 'pastor', 'a herdsman or shepherd', it gives as its second, 'a shepherd of souls; specially the minister in charge of a church or congregation, with particular reference to the spiritual care of his "flock" '. Involved in both definitions is the sense of unquestioned authority, albeit one which is primarily expressed and received as care.

What do we feel about such a notion? We may feel, like the boy in the film, that it would be better to shut the door altogether on a world in which people can exercise and be subject to such authority. Perhaps we should stop using the word 'pastor', as belonging irretrievably to that world and not ours? Nevertheless we hesitate before closing the door completely, conscious of what we might lose in the process, especially the rich discussion about authority and care within the Bible itself, carried out through this imagery of shepherds and shepherding.

GOD ALONE

When we look at the biblical material about pastors and pastoring, we are immediately made aware of one major constraint on those who claim such authority. That is, that the title 'shepherd' properly belongs to God alone. In the Old Testament, it is only with caution that the title is used of Israel's human leaders, in contrast to its common use among neighbouring nations.

There are numerous references to God as shepherd in the Psalms, besides the most famous of all in Psalm 23. The opening of Psalm 80: 'Hear, O thou Shepherd of Israel, thou that leadest Joseph like a sheep' (BCP) is just one other example. In the prophecies dating from the time of the Exile, it is also given prominence as a description of God's care for his people.

> Behold, the Lord comes with might,
>   and his arm rules for him;
>   behold, his reward is with him,
>   and his recompense before him.
> He will feed his flock like a shepherd,
>   he will gather the lambs in his arms,
> he will carry them in his bosom,
>   and gently lead those that are with young.
>   (Isaiah 40: 10–11 RSV)

For us nowadays, to speak of people as being like sheep is to demean them. But in the Hebrew scriptures, the term 'God's flock' is a term of special honour. It denotes Israel's sense of election as well as of dependence: 'We are his people, and the sheep of his pasture' (Psalm 100, BCP). This sense of special intimacy with God is focused particularly in the historical remembrance of the Exodus and the settlement in the Promised Land. As Psalm 78 puts it:

> He smote all the first-born in Egypt,
>   the first issue of their strength in the tents of Ham.
> Then he led forth his people like sheep,
>   and guided them in the wilderness like a flock.

He led them to safety, so that they were not afraid;
  but the sea overwhelmed their enemies.
And he brought them to his holy land,
  to the mountain which his right hand had won.
He drove out nations before them:
  he apportioned them for a possession
  and settled the tribes of Israel in their tents.

(Psalm 78: 51–55 RSV)

Those who have a special place in God's faithfulness to his
covenant with his people also merit the title of shepherd,
especially Moses and David. 'Thou leadest thy people like
sheep: by the hand of Moses and Aaron' (Psalm 77: 20 BCP),
says the psalmist; and when the people of Israel make their
covenant with David at Hebron they say: 'In time past, when
Saul was king over us, it was you that led out and brought
in Israel; and the Lord said to you, "You shall be shepherd
of my people Israel, and you shall be prince over Israel" ' (2
Samuel 5: 2 RSV). It is not merely a historical detail that
Moses is given his call at the Burning Bush when he is guarding sheep (Exodus 3: 1ff.), and that David, equally, is taken
from the sheepfolds (Psalm 78: 70–72). This is one way in
which the analogy is made between their leadership of Israel
and God's.

But the primary relationship implied in the terms
'shepherd' and 'shepherding' remains that between God and
his flock, Israel. This is experienced primarily in the whole
community's sense of calling under the terms of the covenant
God has made with them. Human leaders are lent authority
by God only in so far as they serve to sustain and revive this
sense of calling. This is an important point to grasp when
talking about forms of leadership in the Church. Israel's sense
of election, her sense of being God's flock, comes before the
setting up of any system of human leadership. Space is created
for human leadership only in so far as it serves the covenant
relationship, a relationship which has been set up, first of all,
by God's grace, which made a nation out of slaves, liberating
them to lead a new life in community.

Furthermore, authority lent by God to those who become
shepherds under him makes them more accountable to him,

not only for their own behaviour, but for those they are supposed to guide, as the stories of Moses and David show. When
the people test God's patience at Meribah, forcing him to
perform the miracle of bringing water out of the rock, God
holds Moses responsible for sharing the people's lack of faith
and swears that he will not be allowed to enter the Promised
Land with them (Numbers 20: 1–13). David shows the same
sense of personal responsibility when he asks God to strike
him rather than the people he believes are being punished
because of his failure as a shepherd in numbering them for
the purposes of taxation: 'These sheep, what have they done?
Let thy hand, I pray thee, be against me and my father's
house' (2 Samuel 24: 17 RSV).

PROPHETIC CRITICISM

If leaders like Moses and David are not immune from God's
wrath on occasion, how much less so are those run-of-the-mill
leaders, the kings, priests, prophets and prominent people
who are so often the object of prophetic diatribe, in Isaiah,
Jeremiah, Ezekiel and the lesser prophets. In these diatribes,
the title 'shepherd', far from confirming human authority,
questions it by contrast with God's faithfulness to Israel as
the true shepherd of the flock. 'Wail, you shepherds,' says
Jeremiah, 'and cry, and roll in ashes, you lords of the flock,
for the days of your slaughter and dispersion have come, and
you shall fall like choice rams' (Jeremiah 25:34 RSV).

It is not that the prophets disregard the authority of Israel's
leaders. They share in a divinely ordained task of leadership,
which the prophets accept is shown not only in their care for
the flock, especially its weakest members, but in the power
they exercise over them in judgement. But, under the terms
set up by God himself in the covenant, the distinction between
these different aspects of their task is actually very slight.
God's power and righteousness is known precisely in the protection of the rights of the weak against the strong. Rulers
who exercise their authority wrongly, without fear of God and
regard for the flock, transgress the limits set on all human
authority by God's covenant, a covenant whose very basis is

reciprocity. In doing so they bring disaster not only on themselves but on the whole people.

The two most interesting passages in this respect are Ezekiel 34 and Zechariah 10–11 and 13: 7–9. Again, it is the provisional and temporary nature of all human leadership which is referred to. The first passage speaks of Israel's rulers as hirelings who prey on the sheep, thus anticipating Jesus' words in John 10: 7–19, and goes on to speak of the return from Exile, as a reassertion by God of his own role as Shepherd of Israel.

> I myself will be the shepherd of my sheep, and I will make them lie down, says the Lord God. I will seek the lost, and I will bring back the strayed, and I will bind up the crippled, and I will strengthen the weak, and the fat and the strong I will watch over [the Hebrew text has 'destroy']; I will feed them in justice. (Ezekiel 34: 15–16 RSV)

After they have been brought back, God will set up one shepherd, 'my servant David' (vv. 23–24). But only in order to establish an ever greater sense of intimacy between God and his people under a new covenant. This is underlined in the last verse of the chapter: 'And you, my sheep, are the flock I shall pasture, and I am your God – it is the Lord Yahweh who speaks' (v. 31 JB).

In the second passage, from Zechariah, the prophet himself is pictured as a shepherd, whose service God deliberately withdraws from the flock as a punishment. 'Strike the shepherd, that the sheep may be scattered', says Zechariah 13: 7b (a phrase remembered by the synoptic Gospels in their passion narratives). Again future restoration is pictured in terms of God's direct rule over his people:

> They will call on my name,
>   and I will answer them.
> I will say, 'They are my people';
>   and they will say, 'the Lord is my God.'
>   (Zechariah 13: 9b RSV)

Summing up, we could say that, though the Old Testament

gives no room for democratic checks on leadership within the context of the covenant, severe constraints are nevertheless placed on it. Only in so far as it reflects and mediates God's own shepherding of his people under the covenant, has it any real authority, and it works towards its own demise in a future time when God's call will be obeyed without the need for any human intermediaries.

IDENTIFICATION, RESPONSIBILITY AND RISK

Several reflections on the pastoral ministry arise out of this material. The first is about identification. Professional carers of all kinds are constantly being cautioned about the dangers of over-identification with their clients. We are warned that if we become too emotionally involved there is a danger that we will lose our impartiality, that we will forget the codes laid down for professional behaviour and get sucked in. If this happens, then our authority as professionals will be compromised and we will be unable to help.

The biblical material suggests a different model of involvement, based on a belief in divine behaviour. God himself is not uninvolved. He does not engage with his creation as an unmoved mover. He is as warmly involved as is a nomadic shepherd with his sheep. He totally identifies himself with the needs of his people. That is why, in the scriptures, he is so angry with the shepherds, the leaders of Israel, when they mislead his flock. If God's behaviour is not, in that sense, impartial, but based on a passionate identification with his people, then the same is expected of the leaders he appoints over them.

The relationship between the shepherd and the flock is a matter of life and death. One of the contexts in which Israel's leaders are most often spoken of as shepherds is warfare. In this context we perhaps see most clearly the way in which leadership, identification and self sacrifice are bound together. Sometimes Israel is pictured as an army being led into battle, sometimes as a people wandering in the wilderness, sometimes as a new nation trying to live at peace with her neighbours. But in all these contexts, the leaders are being invited by God into a costly relationship, not only with those they lead, but with God himself, who remains, in the last analysis, the only true Lord of hosts, shepherd in the wilderness, and divine husbandman.

Secondly, identification brings with it accountability, but not in the way that we more usually think of the latter today. It is not based on maintaining a certain standard in the performance of professional services, a form of limited accountability, but on a potentially unlimited sense of solidarity. Just as it is impossible for God to be over-identified with his people, so the same is true for anyone given authority, either as a prince, priest or prophet within the community God has created. Being held accountable for one another is one aspect of the biblical understanding of community as it arises from God's own act of identification and solidarity with people as their redeemer.

Finally, the biblical understanding of pastoral leadership is heavily impregnated with a sense of risk. Modern professional modes of caring seek to reduce the level of risk, both to the professional and the client, by enforcing conformity to a professional code of behaviour. At one level, we can draw a parallel between this and the biblical injunction to those in authority to remain true to the norms set out in the written word of the Law. But beneath this is another level of understanding, which is that God himself has taken the risk of identifying his own honour with the fortunes of his people. God, as it were, risks his reputation on his people's obedience to the agreement he has made with them, an obedience which is potential rather than actual. Therefore anyone who is put in the position of disclosing God's faithfulness in leadership is open to the same dimension of risk. Because the outcome of God's commitment is not yet certain, to come between God and his people as a leader is inevitably to accept the risk of incurring anger, misunderstanding and rejection.

This sense of risk is intrinsic to the biblical imagery. To be a shepherd is to be God's fellow worker in leading his people in the wilderness, keeping watch over them, anticipating their needs, keeping them on the move. The Bible's understanding of God's relationship with his people under the terms of the covenant is a dynamic one. It is always breaking down, being renewed and opened up to a greater fulfilment. This carries with it the corollary that any pattern of ministry and leadership which encourages people to settle down rather than stay on the move is liable to become obstructive. To use modern jargon, the biblical understanding of pastoring is proactive rather than reactive. It is not a matter of keeping people where they are, but of keeping pace with God where he is leading.

3

THE GOOD SHEPHERD

IT IS IMPOSSIBLE to understand the messiahship of Jesus without taking into account the Old Testament background which contrasts the shepherding of God with the failure of human leadership. Jesus himself declares that he has been sent by God to the lost sheep of Israel (Matthew 10: 6). In his mission he reveals the divine compassion for his people as sheep without a shepherd, by healing their diseases, but also by going around the cities and villages, teaching in their synagogues and preaching the gospel of the kingdom (Matthew 9: 35–38). His ministry fulfils the expectation of the prophets that God will make himself directly responsible for the leadership of his people. What Israel experienced of God in the exodus from Egypt is remembered and transformed in the ministry of Jesus, which results in a new liberation, including Gentiles this time, as well as Jews.

The writer to the Hebrews refers to this ministry of Jesus when he ends his epistle with these words:

> Now may the God of peace who brought again from the dead our Lord Jesus, the great shepherd of the sheep, by the blood of the eternal covenant, equip you with everything good that you may do his will, working in you that which is pleasing in his sight, through Jesus Christ; to whom be glory for ever and ever. Amen. (Hebrews 13: 20–21 RSV)

As the writer makes clear, it is a ministry which finds its fulfilment in the cross. There the themes of identification, responsibility and risk, which we picked up at the end of the last chapter as characteristic of the ministry of leadership shared with God, are brought together in Christ's one sacrifice of himself, once offered, which makes him, again in the words of the writer to the Hebrews, 'the pioneer and perfecter of our faith' (Hebrews 12: 2 RSV). In the power of the Holy Spirit, Jesus' ministry extends beyond the grave. He remains the one true 'apostle and high priest of our profession' (Hebrews 3: 1 KJV). The Church needs no system of leadership and pattern of ministry in addition to that; but it is the task of ministries within the Church to disclose it in various ways. The shepherding of Christ, known in a shared calling (cf. Hebrews 12: 1), is both intimate and challenging. The pastoral ministry points most clearly to that ministry when it shares these qualities.

The classic description of Jesus' ministry as shepherd is found in John 10. His sense of calling to this ministry, his full acceptance of the demand for identification, responsibility and risk, in contrast to the refusal of Israel's former leaders castigated by the prophets, is all concentrated in his statement, 'I am the good shepherd. The good shepherd lays down his life for the sheep' (John 10:11 RSV).

A leap of imagination is required to recall the conditions in which a nomadic shepherd works outside an enclosed field system and without dogs. The relationship between shepherd and sheep established in these conditions is very intimate. The control of the shepherd over the sheep comes as much from familiarity on both sides, as it does from any authority held over against them. Hence the emphasis in John 10 on the shepherd's voice as something intimate, distinctive and personal: 'The sheep hear his voice, and he calls his own sheep by name and leads them out. When he has brought out all his own, he goes before them, and the sheep follow him, for they know his voice . . . I am the good shepherd; I know my own and my own know me' (vv. 3, 4 and 14 RSV). The intimacy of the relationship is emphasized in the rest of the Gospels as well, though there the emphasis is more on the lengths to which the shepherd will go in order to seek out his sheep and bring back the lost (cf. Matthew 18: 12ff. and Luke 15: 4f.).

The characteristic position of the shepherd in relation to the flock suggested by the passage is going in front of it, anticipating danger, not, as a picture drawn from English farming life might suggest, behind it. The image includes, therefore, an idea of the common acceptance of risk and the sharing of dangers by the shepherd and the flock. When the collect from the Book of Common Prayer speaks of the grace of God 'preventing', i.e. 'going before' us, it exactly captures the quality of care suggested by this picture of the shepherd ahead of his flock, putting himself at risk to anticipate danger to the flock.

When the nomadic shepherd has found a place where there is pasture, often after wandering a great distance, he must let the flock disperse in order to feed there. At nightfall, as referred to in the John 10 passage, he calls the sheep and leads them to a sheepfold, if one is available, where he remains at the threshold to make sure nothing gets in or out. In the morning he counts them out, as in the evening he had counted them in. If there is no sheepfold he is forced to keep watch out in the open against night predators. The bond created between the shepherd and the sheep, could not therefore be closer. This is recalled again in John 17, in the passage known as Jesus' high priestly prayer for his followers, when he says:

> I am not praying for the world but for those whom thou has given me, for they are thine; all mine are thine, and thine are mine, and I am glorified in them . . . While I was with them, I kept them in thy name, which thou hast given me; I have guarded them, and none of them is lost but the son of perdition, that the scriptures might be fulfilled. (John 17: 9–10,12 RSV)

These passages provide important clues to the nature of pastoral ministry. Pastoral ministry is not merely reactive. There is a dimension of challenge and risk in pastoral relationships as well as one of comfort. On the communal level, it involves taking initiatives, anticipating dangers, protecting the weak from the strong, keeping an eye on developments, watching and waiting. But however active or permissive, forceful or gentle, the pastoral relationship is in a particular context, it is always based on a network of personal trust and knowledge, shared by the community as a whole.

PASTORS AND EVANGELISTS

In moving from the Old Testament references about shepherds to those associated with the ministry of Jesus in the New, we are aware of a transformation in its meaning, as in other titles involving a claim to authority – 'Son of God', 'Lord', 'High Priest' – in the light of his ministry of self-offering culminating in the cross. The authority of the shepherd over against the flock – a strong theme in the Old Testament – is submerged in the New. One thing that does not change, however, is the thrust of the imagery towards understanding the future needs as well as the present life of the community as the focus for the pastoral task. This context for understanding the imagery in the Old and the New Testaments remains the connection between the themes of nomadic shepherding and wandering in the wilderness – or pilgrimage.

This brings the pastoral task into closer association with other tasks of the Church, such as evangelism, which are also concerned with the future as well as the present. The modern distinction between the work of the pastor and the work of evangelism is foreign to the Bible. Both forms of ministry imply a willingness to change, and a movement from one kind of life to another. The distinction between the pastoral task and evangelism impoverishes *both* aspects of ministry. So much evangelism is carried out as if it had nothing to do with human flourishing. And so much pastoring is carried out within a very small circle of people, without any real hope of change, when the whole thrust of the biblical material is towards calling those who are lost and left outside.

Evangelizing and pastoring are not successive stages in the development of the Church. We do not leave the one behind in order to pursue the other. In the story of the Exodus, God's act of pastoring in calling his people out of Egypt precedes his proclamation of the Torah (which one might call the good news of the Old Testament) in the desert. If the focus is to be on change and liberation, then evangelism and pastoral care may be seen as aspects of the same ministry. We can go as far as to say that one form of activity is not really possible without the other. Both are concerned with the move towards a better life. The reason why many pastors have wished to distance themselves from 'evangelism', so-called, is that the word has become associated with defective and coercive methods of persuasion which imprison people rather than liberate them. What we do not always realize is that some forms of pastoring or 'shepherding' can be equally manipulative, and destructive of real human growth.

GOD'S FAITHFULNESS, SHEPHERDING AND LIBERATION

The ministry of Jesus completes the movement towards liberation begun with God's call to the patriarchs, the first who were called by God to a nomadic existence. As the promised messianic shepherd, Jesus leads his followers out of the old fold of Judaism into a new covenant. The intimacy of God with his people, an intimacy set up from the start by his total concern and faithfulness towards them, is sealed by the offering of life by his Son.

The theme of identification is begun in the Old Testament, where the God of the covenant is also the defender of the poor, the widow and the fatherless, who judges the faithfulness of the leaders of the community to the covenant by their behaviour towards such people. This theme is completed when the Son of Man himself becomes one of the poor. From this point onwards, the needs of the poor, their claim to attention and service, cannot be distinguished from the worship due to God. Their lack of power, freedom and authority becomes, paradoxically, the means of revealing the divine claim upon all of us. It reveals the divine humility and, at the same time, how different divine power, freedom and authority is from human pretensions to power and claims to competence based on birth, status or learning.

> Not every one who says to me, 'Lord, Lord,' shall enter the kingdom of heaven, but he who does the will of my Father who is in heaven. On that day many will say to me, 'Lord, Lord, did we not prophesy in your name, and cast out demons in your name, and do many mighty works in your name?' And then I will declare to them,

'I never knew you; depart from me you evildoers.'
(Matthew 7: 21–23 RSV)

There is continuity with the Old Testament in that Jesus shares in the divine authority which judges all forms of human leadership. At the same time there is a decisive change in the language, brought about by the confrontation between human and divine authority in the passion of Jesus and the change of context for discussion about leadership, from affairs of state in the Old Testament prophecy, to matters of order and well-being among newly established congregations in the New. In this new context, brought about by the Messiah's death and resurrection, every exercise of authority is at the same time an act of service, whether it is keeping order in worship, exhortation, challenge, or even confrontation. Even in the case of excommunication, in the New Testament this is a pastoral decision, undertaken for a limited period for the future good of the individual as well as the community. If the exercise of authority loses that character and becomes oppressive, or forgets the needs of God's little ones, it automatically loses its conformity to Christ.

THE LAST JUDGEMENT

All authority in the New Testament is understood as a kind of ministry, even judgement. In the parable of the Last Judgement in Matthew 25: 31–46, the Son of Man is pictured as a shepherd dividing the sheep from the goats. But his judgement is based on how they in turn have done justice to others pastorally, in supplying the needs of the hungry, the thirsty, the stranger, the naked, the sick and the imprisoned. He has met them already in these little ones, the least of the brethren. The implications for ministry within and outside the community of believers are manifold. Jürgen Moltmann writes of this passage in his book, *The Church in the Power of the Spirit*:

Where is the true church? In the fellowship manifest in word and sacrament, or in the latent brotherhood of the Judge hidden in the poor? . . . The Christian church in its manifest form has always appealed to the exalted

Christ's promises of authority, interpreting itself as the body of the exalted Lord, The apocalyptic Christ, the poor, hungry, forsaken Judge, has generally remained outside the door of church and society.[1]

In the ministry that Jesus shares with his followers it is impossible to distinguish entirely between the proclamation of the gospel in evangelism and serving human needs in pastoral action. Faced with a question about his messiahship from John's disciples, Jesus replies, 'Go and tell John what you hear and see: the blind receive their sight and the lame walk, lepers are cleansed and the deaf hear, and the dead are raised up, and the poor have the good news preached to them' (Matthew 11: 4–5 RSV). The basis of all ministry is compassion, in response to the passionate identification of God with the needs of his own creation. In the ministry of Jesus, evangelism and pastoral care both have the same motive, and the same goal, which is the preparation of individuals and whole communities for the coming of God's kingdom.

> When he saw the crowds, he had compassion for them because they were harassed and helpless, like sheep without a shepherd. Then he said to his disciples, 'The harvest is plentiful, but the labourers are few; pray therefore the Lord of the harvest to send out labourers to his harvest.' (Matthew 9: 36–38 RSV)

In the ministry of Jesus no distinction is made between preaching the kingdom, making the hungry sit down to eat (cf. Mark 6: 34ff.), and healing infirmities. All alike are forms of compassionate service. Too often, in disagreements about how to serve the gospel, the lines are drawn up between those who regard evangelism in order to save people for a totally spiritual salvation as the only proper task of the Church, and those who see pastoral service in imitation of Christ as the only form of authentic witness, to be preferred to open proclamation. The New Testament is not aware of these distinctions. Having made the identification between the exalted Christ of the Church and the poor, apocalyptic Christ, using the parable in Matthew 25, Moltmann goes on to apply it to this contemporary disagreement about evangelism and pastoral action:

> If Matthew 25 is applied to the teaching and practice of the church, then the conflict between a 'dogmatic' and an 'ethical' Christianity must be resolvable. Statements about the 'manifest' and 'latent' church could also be understood in the sense of the double presence and brotherhood of Christ. Admittedly one could not then simply talk about a 'Christianity outside the church' or about 'the workings of the Spirit outside the church'. For then the question is not how people or happenings outside the church respond to the church, but how the church responds to the presence of Christ in those who are 'outside', hungry, thirsty, sick, naked and imprisoned. *It is not a question of the integration of Christians outside the church into Christianity in its ecclesiastical form; it is a matter of the church's integration in Christ's promised presence: Ubi Christus, ibi ecclesia.*[2]

This is a very exciting passage, and one that shows the true relationship between pastoral action and evangelism. Both find their fulfilment in following the mission of God to the world, and his pilgrimage within it in the person of the Incarnate One. This is fully and finally revealed when the identification of the promised Messiah with suffering humanity reaches its crisis and apogee in his self-emptying on the cross.

The locus of divine activity is not only in the community of believers which anticipates in its worship the final defeat of evil and death. Nor is it only in the mystery of the suffering of the poor left outside. Where the two meet is the place where God is most truly known. *Ubi Christus, ibi ecclesia.* The Church cannot claim to be the Church if it remains in an island of complacency with the exalted Christ while the world goes to the devil. Nor is it truly the Church if it only acts out of a sense of its own fullness, because the movement of God towards the world is a divine outpouring in which nothing is held back.

'ART THOU HE?'

I love the Advent Responsory as set to music by Palestrina. The choir used to sing it at the doors of the chapel before the Advent carol services at Kings College London when I was chaplain there, and I always found it an intensely dramatic moment. There was the Church, as it were, gathered together in the chapel for a great institutional occasion, and here was the call of the Messiah, the one who stands at the door and knocks (Revelation 3: 20). The responsory is: 'Go ye out to meet him and say, "Tell us, art thou he that shall come to reign over thy people Israel?" ' It is a command which recalls so much from Scripture: the call to Abraham to go out and leave his own people; the call to the people of Israel to leave Egypt and meet God in the wilderness; the call to leave a land corrupted to endure a purifying exile, and the call to return; the King's command to his servants in the parable to go out into the highways and byways to invite the poor to his banquet because he wants his house to be full; the call to go out to all nations and make them disciples.

Without the obedience to the command, 'Go ye out', the messiahship of Jesus, the Suffering Servant, cannot be known. When we meet him in this way in the darkness and confusion of a world still in the process of becoming, our first locution must be a question, not a statement, because his messiahship can only be fully known when his exalted headship of the Church is brought together with his hidden presence in the mystery of the world's suffering and coming to be.

The cross decisively alters the context for all exercise of authority. All the titles ascribed to Jesus, including that of the messianic Shepherd, are transformed by the fact of his death. They do not become any less authoritative, but their authority is encountered in a radically different way.

> Jesus called them to him and said, 'You know that in the world the recognized rulers lord it over their subjects, and their great men make them feel the weight of authority. That is not the way with you; among you, whoever wants to be great must be your servant, and whoever wants to be first must be the willing slave of all. For even

the Son of Man did, not come to be served but to serve, and to give up his life as a ransom for many.' (Mark 10: 42–45 NEB)

This is a command affecting the behaviour of the whole people of God in the exercise of their corporate responsibilities, evangelical and pastoral, towards those outside the community of faith, as well a command determining behaviour towards one another within it. In St Paul's letters, all forms of authority are also forms of service, including that of apostle. This is because they have an internal as well as an external aspect, which is to live in growing conformity with Christ's death in order to share his resurrection. Thus he can say of his own struggles on behalf of the gospel: 'While we live we are always being given up to death for Jesus' sake, so that the life of Jesus may be manifested in our mortal flesh. So death is at work in us, but life in you' (2 Corinthians 4: 11–12 RSV).

Modern commentators emphasize once again how Paul, while insisting that the decisive event had already occurred in the coming of the Lord Jesus Christ, also looks towards a final imminent fulfilment. The statement 'Jesus Christ is Lord, to the glory of God the Father (Philippians 2: 11)' is a confession of faith still awaiting fulfilment. It is no accident that it occurs in the most famous passage describing the incarnation as divine self-emptying in order to become obedient to the depths of human need to the extent of death on a cross. Elsewhere Paul describes this divine initiative more succinctly as a becoming poor, in order to make us rich (2 Corinthians 8: 9). The Church is meant to follow the path opened up by that divine self-emptying in a mission which includes active proclamation and service.

Paul does not distinguish between an ethical task shown forth in service and a dogmatic task shown forth in proclamation, any more than Jesus does in his own ministry in the Gospels. The famous statements I have just referred to, from Philippians 2 and 2 Corinthians 8, which have become dogmatic proof texts for a 'kenotic' Christology, occur in the context of the apostle's request for *ethical* behaviour on the part of the community he is writing to. In Philippians 2 this is to be expressed in mutual forbearance and service within the congregation; in 2 Corinthians 8, by joining in the collection Paul is organizing for the needs of the saints in Jerusalem.

In the latter case, Paul saw his collection as being a task required by prophecy which was to herald the final end, thus making it truly impossible to distinguish ethically inspired service from proclamation. Similarly, Paul sees the grace of discerning the body of Christ in the eucharist and proclaiming the death of the Lord until he comes, not as a matter of intellectual illumination, but of ethical behaviour by sharing wealth with those who have nothing rather than making a parade of it (1 Corinthians 11: 17–34).

I wonder how much we have lost in making the sorts of distinction we now take for granted between the ethical and the dogmatic, the pastoral and the evangelistic. For most of us, pastoral work has become a matter of the routine maintenance of congregational life, which we keep in a separate compartment from theological reflection on the one hand, and the task of evangelism on the other. Often we see it as a duty invested in particular individuals commissioned and trained for it, and not as a command laid upon the community as a whole. If pastoral work *is* seen as going outside the confines of the congregation, then it is usually in terms of maintaining a presence in society generally, or setting an example. It is seldom seen as a matter of taking risks or initiatives. For this reason it does not present the Church with the challenge of sharing the passionate identification of God with the lost, the fallen, the weak and the rejected. Sheila Cassidy has written in her book *Sharing the Darkness*, subtitled 'The Spirituality of Caring':

> In the story of the Good Shepherd the virtuous are left singing hymns in church while the shepherd goes out into the hills or down the dark alleys of the inner city to search out and bring back in triumph the one who was lost. This is the God I meet in the gospels and the God I meet in pastors who seem to me worthy of the name. It is the God who has come to save not the virtuous but the sinner.[3]

It is hard to distinguish the sort of pastoring to which she refers, undertaken out of a strong faith in the gracious initiative God has taken with all of us, from evangelism. Pastoral care of this kind is at the same time a statement of faith in God's future kingdom and a search for the truth of his presence and purpose hidden in creation. Every offering of pastoral care, every service to the gospel and every exercise of leadership should be tested against the background of God's shepherding of the *whole* of creation, and not just of the Church. Even evangelism, if it is not undertaken in the spirit of compassion – if it does not, in other words, have a pastoral heart – ceases to be evangelism. For:

> Man's compassion extends to his neighbour,
> > but the compassion of the Lord extends to everything
> > > that lives;
> rebuking, correcting, and teaching,
> > bringing them back as a shepherd brings his flock.
> He has compassion on those who accept correction,
> > and who fervently look for judgements.
> > > > > > (Ecclesiasticus 18: 12–14 JB)

4

PASTORS AND PRIESTS

IN THE LIGHT of the discussion in the previous chapters we are able to give a definition of what we think pastoral activity is. Pastoral activity is purposive, not reactive. It is undertaken trusting that God is present in the community of faith and in our experience of the world, and it works towards the coming of his kingdom. It is an activity meant to provoke change rather than maintain stability. Its medium is faith, not the competence of its ministers. It is most effective and most productive of change where the sense of the presence of God is most alive and sensitive. Every pastoral encounter, therefore, has a twofold aspect, active and passive. On one level it is an intervention on behalf of something yet to be fully revealed, that has to be worked for. At another level it is a matter of making space for something which is already present, dynamically at work, and demands patience, watchfulness and self-surrender.

One person who understood this was the seventeenth-century priest and poet, George Herbert. In his book *A Priest to the Temple* he gives what we would now consider an entirely traditional picture of the seventeenth-century parson. Indeed, the book was important in helping to create the persona of the Anglican clergyman as a gentle and condescending father figure, slightly on the edge of events, but nevertheless someone carrying significance for the whole community.

Nobody can deny that we have a lot of difficulty with such a picture today, though it is surprising how it still persists in the modern imagination, as many novels, poems and articles bear witness. Is this merely nostalgia which the Church has outgrown, but society, or certain sections of it, has not? Or does the picture put us in contact with communal sources of memory and imagination which are still important for the pastoral ministry however it is carried out, whether by a single figure in a village of a few hundred in the seventeenth century or a team of people working among the anonymous crowd in the city today?

There is more than one way of reading Herbert's book. We need to remember that he was writing in a period of intense religious excitement and conflict, when many different models of the Church were being advocated by different groups. His book is a sustained piece of argument for a form of ministry open to the world but undertaken in pursuit of goals that went beyond it, and it emphasizes the power of personal example as a way of communicating common ideals. It is also an apology for the course he had taken in his own life by rejecting the world of the court, a world for which he was naturally suited by birth and talent, for a world which was initially much more strange to him, that of a country clergyman in Wiltshire. At the heart of the book is an understanding of the call of God as requiring a total commitment in which nothing is held back by the pastor from God or the flock. It is the description of an ideal towards which Herbert strove in his own life, and which still has the power to hold our attention.

A PRIEST TO THE TEMPLE

Herbert makes it clear at the beginning of his book that it is an exercise in practical spirituality in which he is setting before himself as well as others a picture of a totally dedicated life. Hence the book's subtitle, 'The Country Parson, his Character, and Rule of Holy Life'.

> Being desirous (through the mercy of God) to please Him, for Whom I am and live, and Who giveth my desires and performances; and considering with myself that the way to please Him is to feed my flock diligently and faithfully, since our Saviour hath made that the argument of a pastor's love, I have resolved to set down the form and character of a true pastor, that I may have

a mark to aim at, which also I will set as high as I can, since he shoots higher that threatens the moon, than he that aims at a tree.

The book begins with an uncompromising statement of the pastor's task which recalls much of what we have already found in the biblical witness:

> A pastor is the deputy of Christ, for the reducing of man to the obedience of God. This definition is evident, and contains the direct steps of pastoral duty and authority.

Implicit in this statement is an eschatological understanding of pastoral activity. The pastor's efforts are bent towards preparing, not just individuals but a whole community, for the coming of Christ.

However the element of authority *over* the flock is immediately balanced in the opening paragraph by an equally uncompromising definition of the priest as a minister, quoting Colossians 1: 24 that he 'fills up that which is behind of the afflictions of Christ in his flesh, for His body's sake, which is the Church'. Again, this definition has an eschatological thrust, concentrating as it does on the 'travail' of the Church which must continue until the end. Thus Herbert sees that the priest's 'dignity', i.e. his authority, cannot be distinguished from his 'duty' or service 'to do that which Christ did, and after His manner, both for doctrine and life'. The theme of identification as the prerequisite for a truly pastoral ministry is again very strong here as it is in the biblical witness. The pastor is personally completely identified with his role, and the role demands of him complete identification with the needs of his flock.

This theme of identification is brought out in many areas. For example, in discussing the parson's knowledge in chapter 4, Herbert asks that the parson should be full of all knowledge which pertains to the life of his country parishioners, even tillage and pasturage. That way he can use their life experience to lead them into knowledge of God 'because people by what they understand best are best led to what they understand not'. Elsewhere Herbert stresses that the pastor should strive to acquire knowledge in areas that will be useful to his parishioners, particularly in the area of folk medicine, so that he can practise himself on this level, and train others to do so too.

In this way the pastor's knowledge and capacity for learning, which could be used as a barrier to demonstrate a difference in status between himself and the flock, is instead made available as a form of service. This is brought out again in chapter 8 where the pastor is pictured as laying out his wares on a Sunday:

> The Country Parson, as soon as he awakes on Sunday morning, presently falls to work, and seems to himself so as a market man is when market day comes, or a shopkeeper when customers use to come in. His thoughts are full of making the best of the day and contriving it to his best gains.

But in the same image, Herbert suggests, by analogy with the shopkeeper's desire for profit, the purposive nature of the parson's activity, which goes beyond merely responding to the needs and desires of his congregation.

What Herbert advocates suggests the sort of learning dynamic that might go on in many parts of the world today, for example between a health worker, sponsored by a government or international care agency, and local people. The health worker comes into the situation with some general priorities. But she cannot make them real unless she gains the confidence and co-operation of the local people, since it is they who are to be the agents of the hoped-for improvement in health care, not the worker herself, who may only be there for a short time. Her chief means of making this happen is to make her own expertise accessible to the community, whilst at the same time taking account of the traditional knowledge and expertise they have already. To incorporate both sources of knowledge in the same scheme requires a willingness to adapt and a quick eye for any opportunities which present themselves in the local context. The same dynamic informs the theory behind a lot of community development work. In Herbert's understanding, this is understood theologically as an expression of God's concern for the wholeness of life and human dedication to his purposes, and also as a matter of practical rather than theoretical knowledge, drawing on lived experience.

There is, in Herbert's eyes, an area of specialist knowledge which the parson has, namely his knowledge of the Bible. But here again the chief instrument of learning is experience in terms of a 'holy life . . . assuring himself that wicked men, however learned, do not know the Scriptures, because they feel them not'; and prayer, because how are we going to draw from a well so deep if 'we have nothing of ourselves to draw with'? The sort of knowledge suggested here is personal and experiential, and, in principle, open to every believer – knowledge by faith, in other words, or heart-knowledge.

The pastoral nature of the parson's ministry is not, in Herbert's view, defined by the particular professional tasks he is called upon to perform. These may vary, and besides, the non-professional aspects of his life, like his home, his relationship with his family, his hobbies and entertainments, are equally involved. Whatever he is involved in, whether it is preaching, catechizing in the home, almsgiving and visiting the sick, exhorting wrongdoers, or offering hospitality, how it is done is as important as what is done. For example, in catechizing, Herbert prefers the Socratic method as a way of drawing out even the most ignorant so that they gain confidence about the knowledge they have, and emphasizes the parson's patience in this as necessary in one who is in his own way a fellow-labourer, accomplishing what he can by 'set, and laboured, and continued speech'. Or, in practising hospitality, Herbert expects the parson to be as courteous and open to the poor as he is to the rich as a 'diligent observer and tracker of God's ways' (chapter 11).

Herbert is conscious of two strands in his authority as a country parson: a spiritual authority based on his obedience to the task for which he has been ordained – the cure of souls – and the status he enjoys in the social hierarchy, which, being a man of his time, Herbert also sees as being in some sense ordained by God. He is not unaware that in certain circumstances there may be conflict between the two. But both as a spiritual and as a social leader, the parson, in Herbert's view, acts as a focus for powers and abilities which are present more generally in the whole community. The parson's own actions act as a kind of mirror which could help or discourage others in the use of their own powers of healing, persuasion, hospitality, forgiveness, and almsgiving. In this traditional picture of the parson's role, what matters more than his own competence to organize systems of relief or distribute resources is the symbolic force of his actions in reminding others of their own powers and responsibilities. Because the whole structure of local society was based on the recognition of personal status within a hierarchy involving people in various types of reciprocal obligation, the parson's example in the way he carried out his private business as well as his public duties had an important effect on the whole of local society, from top to bottom.

The image, therefore, which Herbert has of the pastor's leadership is extremely patriarchal, but at the same time personal. Herbert uses this image both as a way of sanctioning the parson's authority within the social system prevailing at the time, and also as a way of distinguishing it from other forms of authority, both in the way it is exercised and in its effect.

> The Country Parson is not only a father to his flock but professeth himself thoroughly of the opinion, carrying it about with him as fully as if he had begot his whole parish. And of this he makes great use; for by this means, when any sins, he hateth him not as an officer, but pitieth him as a father. (chapter 16)

For a modern reader this language is strange and alienating. It nevertheless conveys Herbert's awareness that the parson represents a kind of authority which is not commensurate with other forms of authority at work in society, and which may run counter to them, as in this case it runs counter to the rigour of the law.

In another example, Herbert sees the deference the parson owes to those of high status as limited by his duties towards them as a pastor, and the equal or prior claims that others have to his time and attention as such. Traces here of a seventeenth-century version of 'bias to the poor'?

[He] holds the rule that nothing is little in God's service . . . Wherefore neither disdaineth he to enter the poorest cottage, though he even creep into it . . . for both God is there also, and those for whom God died. And so much the rather doth he so, as his access is more comfortable [i.e. of more comfort] than to the rich. (chapter 14)

Herbert also recognizes that the spiritual authority exercised by the parson is more insecure than the authority exercised by others in the social hierarchy, because it depends much more than they do on the expectations and beliefs of those among whom the role is exercised. For this reason a pastor's status has to be negotiated. It cannot be carried out without reference to these expectations and beliefs. Part of the skill of an experienced pastor is being able to discern these expectations and how they can be used. For this reason Herbert commends pleasantness of disposition as a great key to do good, 'because all men shun the company of perpetual severity'. The parson must be all things to all men.

Herbert is aware of how the personal nature of the role is bound to draw accusations of hypocrisy and generate contempt, as well as respect, for: 'he must be despised; because this hath been the portion of God his master, and of God's saints his brethren, and this is foretold that it shall be so until things be no more' (Chapter 18).

Attracting contempt is the corollary of holding authority, since authority is bound to be resented and resisted, especially if it is moral and spiritual and carries no other sanctions. There is not so much difference, after all, between Herbert's seventeenth-century ideal and R. S. Thomas' contemporary picture of the country priest picking his way through the parish:

> Priests have a long way to go.
> The people wait for them to come
> To them over the broken glass
> Of their vows, making them pay
> With their sweat's coinage for their correction.[1]

COMMUNAL EXPECTATIONS AND ROLE PERFORMANCE

Herbert's picture of the parson's role and how he fulfils it is not without analogies in the role performance of other professions today, as the reference already made to community development work makes clear (though Herbert's picture also draws on deeper themes of identification and obedience to a call, which we will touch on again later).

Take the example of a teacher in the classroom. The successful teacher is one who can use the pupils' own openness to learning and desire for firm boundaries to create an atmosphere of discipline and purpose in the classroom which to a large extent the pupils minister among themselves. To do this the teacher often has to act up to the role the pupils initially set up (e.g. the expectation that all teachers are strict) before she can introduce her own particular contribution. In the same way Herbert's pastor acts up to the role he has been assigned by the community in order to gain respect. His obedience to the role in this regard counterbalances the resentment it would otherwise provoke.

Today's teacher has few instruments at her disposal to achieve consensus in the classroom apart from her ability to project a persona which will attract the children and channel their energies positively. The teacher often has to suppress her own feelings in order to maintain this identification with her role. This results in a certain amount of personal pain and inner conflict. For instance, she may not be able to assume common rules of behaviour among pupils coming into school. Some children are already well socialized; other children have built up no stable pattern of interaction either with other children or with adults. It is very difficult for the teacher to know what to respond or appeal to in these often very disruptive pupils who can alternate between complete withdrawal and demand for total attention, and how to balance their needs with those of the other pupils in the class. Add to that the often unrealistic expectations that parents have of what the teachers should be able to do, fuelled sometimes by the parents' own sense of failure and low self-esteem, and we can understand why so many teachers suffer from burn-out and exhaustion.

Faced with all these conflicting demands and expectations, the teacher often feels trapped between her own sense of vocation, i.e., what she came into the classroom to do, and what is actually possible. She creates the illusion of control in the classroom, but in fact has few real sanctions that she can apply to back up her authority – apart, in the last resort, from exclusion, which she would see as a sort of failure. The only instrument she has for gaining acceptance of her own vision of her role is the strength of her example as a model for the behaviour she wishes to promote.

No wonder then that the staffroom becomes a place where people can let off steam and give expression to all their pent-up frustration and resentment at having to be obedient to the demands of their role in the classroom. Anyone coming into the staffroom from outside might be shocked by the language, and jump to the wrong conclusion that the staff are not committed to their task. Sometimes, indeed, the strain of conforming to the role becomes too great for the individual teacher herself and, shocked by what she considers to be her own level of hypocrisy and cynicism about her role, she leaves the profession.

A similar high sense of vocation, a willingness to be identified with and obedient to a role which is not of our own making but to a large extent imposed by other people's expectations and beliefs is, traditionally, even more characteristic of clergy than other professions. This is certainly true of George Herbert's ideal pastor. Herbert is aware that there is an inevitable tension between the parson's high sense of calling, his own capacity to fulfil it, and the space created for it by the expectations and understanding of the role among his parishioners. Practical wisdom and humility is needed in negotiating between these different strands.

Herbert was aware of the problems created for the priest as pastor by his right to tithes and association with civil authority. His book is a plea to his fellow clergy, those at least who were well endowed, not to act oppressively with regard to their privileges, but by acting pastorally to make their resources of learning, wealth and influence more generally available; and an attempt to give those clergy who were poor a proper sense of their own worth as pastoral leaders.

Here he is already attempting to provide an independent, theological justification for the parson's role *apart* from his status as generally legitimated by society. In his view, the pastor was not merely to react to a set of beliefs and expectations about his role which were already present, but actively to promote expectations about God's ministry in human affairs in accordance with a vision which was theological rather than merely social. This is brought out very clearly in the chapter entitled 'The Parson's Consideration of Providence'. In Herbert's eyes, the nature of the parson's involvement was meant to point to the presence of God in human affairs, sustaining, governing, correcting, comforting, and to draw its strength from *that*, rather than from any authority derived merely from social prestige and patronage.

However, the question that never arises in Herbert's discussion is whether or not the parish priest's role as pastoral leader is valuable in itself. Perhaps this was unthinkable (at least for an Anglican!) at a time when there was so much general social reinforcement for the role. But now that most of that general reinforcement has gone and the expectations of the priest himself and of other groups and individuals in relation to the role are so various and often so conflicting, the question becomes both thinkable and urgent.

I wish to argue that the contribution the ordained ministry makes to pastoral ministry within and outside congregations is still valuable. That is, as long as sufficient account is taken of the tremendous changes that have occurred in the pattern of belief within church congregations and in society at large, and of the corresponding effect this has had on the role. As I will elaborate later on, I believe that keeping in healthy contact with one's persona as a parish priest and/or ordained minister is more important than the development of a firm sense of professional identity and function, because it draws on a deeper belief in the spiritual energies and potentialities which God has made generally available to people, and in how the priest's own faithfulness to his or her calling can act to release and channel it.

A SENSE OF THE HOLY

Prior to any consideration of personal competence and function is the community of belief which allows an ordained ministry to be recognized and used. The authority of the ordained to do their job for the community is one which is ascribed to them in trust, rather than one that they can clearly demonstrate in terms of professional knowledge or competence. In many pastoral situations the minister is unable to do anything; but the fact that a situation has been opened up to the presence of someone identified as being close to God is often enough to make a difference. This is a matter of common experience and contributes to the special sense of privilege we sometimes gain in certain pastoral situations as the ordained – a sense of privilege which has nothing to do with social or professional status.

In Georges Bernanos' *Diary of A Country Priest*,[2] as I remember it, this sense of privilege is described as the miracle of the empty hands. In that novel, the young French priest of the title, who is himself in a state of spiritual desolation, is nevertheless able to bring about reconciliation in a bitterly divided family and save someone from cynical despair. The novelist implies that, even though the priest is not fully in control either of his own life or of the pastoral situation he is called to enter, hidden resources of healing are made available simply by the fact of his presence. His simply being there has the effect of making the people he encounters aware of the proximity of the holy, and this in itself is enough to provoke change.

Much of the ordained person's ability to provide pastoral care and leadership depends on our willingness to be something for other people rather than what we can do for them. However alien we may find George Herbert's picture now, it is at least conscious of this fact. Urban T. Holmes, an American Episcopalian writer, claims, 'All research of which I know into the life of a parish shows that the sacramental person, the priest of the community, must be clearly identifiable and responsible if that congregation is to be healthy or even to survive'.[3] A controversial statement, but one which points to the importance of the ordained priest or pastor as an embodied sign of God's care for people.

The statement cannot make sense in any other way. No one could expect to be personally competent to do everything that is required for the health and survival of a congregation. The expectation is rather that the presence of a committed ordained person helps to evoke the competences necessary for health and survival already present in the congregation but unattended to. As Holmes puts it, this is a matter of grace rather than works. Another way of expressing it would be to say, with the sociologists of religion, that churches rely on a form of institutionalized charism as a way of ordering their life.

What we are talking about is the discernment of gifts and of charismatic authority, and this may be patterned differently in different churches. It may not be necessary, for example, that one person should hold the sort of position Holmes suggests. But however it is patterned, this ordering depends on three things, none of which can be totally separated from the others: the gifts and obedience to a sense of calling of an individual; the shared belief of a community; and the individual's gifting by that community to carry a particular significance for it. Clearly, institutionalized charism is not the same thing as professional competence. It is a matter of the role assigned to someone in a system of belief rather than the purely rational expectations one might have of someone to perform a particular function.

This sounds good, but it has its darker side. First, it is not possible to make a person who is carrying this sort of significance for a community, accountable in the same way as one might someone who carries out a professional service. Their effectiveness is determined by what others believe, rather than their functional effectiveness. Secondly, and as a corollary, it is not possible for individual pastoral leaders to limit their sense of responsibility to the performance of professional tasks and duties, or easy for them to distinguish between a 'private' self and a professional role. The strong theme of identification and accountability, which we have already identified in the biblical witness, prevents them from being able to distance themselves from their role and contain it. That is why so many of them are prone to overwork and make too little provision for their own needs and the needs of those closest to them, as against the needs of the congregation or parish. Thirdly, pastors cannot protect themselves from the expectations and projections individuals make on to them by pointing out the limits of their professional competence. The pastor's ability to act at all depends on the context created by shared belief. If belief is not present, the pastor's role disappears or is distorted.

The variety of often contradictory expectations and projections made today upon those clearly labelled as religious people, by ordination or in some other way, is one of the major motives behind the desire of clergy to find professional role definitions using models drawn from outside the religious sphere – from management, social work and counselling. But these projections and expectations, whose ultimate source and reference is not the individual pastor at all but the sense of God which the pastor's presence helps to evoke, are the only medium we may use to establish pastoral contact and communication. Sometimes these projections and expectations may be damaging to a person, or frightening – for example when someone in sickness says, 'Vicar, I think God must be punishing me for something I've done wrong.' But they cannot be rejected at the outset, as if something else must be put in their place before the *real* business of ministry can begin. They must be accepted and negotiated before any change can take place.

5

THE LURE OF PROFESSIONALISM

THE MOST DIFFICULT question I was asked at my selection conference for the ordained ministry was, 'Why do you want to be a priest rather than a social worker?' I was still at university and had had little experience outside the field of education. Nor could I say that I had had a definite point of conversion or calling to the priesthood which had carried with it a clear sense of the special nature of the ministry. My sense of vocation had simply been a growing conviction that this was the right thing to do. What had influenced me most was the pastoral example of one or two individual priests who had ministered to me, and I was motivated to put myself forward, in part, by the idealistic assumption that I would be able to help and bring comfort to people too.

My confusion in the face of the question betrayed a certain innocence about the helping professions. It would not have occurred to me then, for example, that social workers are obedient to statutory regulations laid down in law, which often come into conflict with the general aim of helping people; and that their intervention – when carrying out a care order, for example – is often experienced as interference. The desire to help people seemed to me to be sufficient justification in itself. I did not stop to distinguish between the different sorts of help that might be offered. Nor was I able to examine precisely where my desire to help people came from in my own psychological make-up. I have lost some of that innocence now. In particular I have become aware that each profession is obedient to its own rules and purposes, and that the helping image of any professional role sometimes masks an unequal struggle about who has the authority to make judgements between the client and the professional, even when the whole *raison d'être* of the role is one of service.

Let me give an example of how the way in which professionals work on their own ground demonstrates the particular professional philosophy to which they conform. Sheila Cassidy, who is a doctor herself, describes in *Sharing the Darkness* how the conventions of the doctor's surgery often serve to strip the patient of his own resources of knowledge and personal dignity. The long wait to be seen, the request to take off his clothes to be examined, the long pauses while the doctor peruses the patient's notes and writes things down, all serve to demonstrate to the patient the unequal position he or she is in. It is argued that the reason for these conventions is to make as clear a space as possible for the doctor's clinical judgement, which is objective and scientific, and therefore, in that sense, impersonal. But this is not the whole story. It *is* true that the sequence often serves to minimize the patient's contribution to the diagnosis, in particular what the patient has to *say* about the problem, in contrast to what the doctor can *see*. The hidden assumption is that what the patient has to say about himself is not a very important part of making a diagnosis, though this is contradicted time and time again in actual practice. This assumption is only possible because of the belief that the doctor has access, through professional training, to resources for clinical judgement which are unaffected by the precise circumstances of personal encounter with the patient. But this is not the case.

Everybody has at least one tale of the surgery or consulting room which illustrates this. Here is one. A dustman in his fifties bruised himself at work but became alarmed when the soreness did not go away. His local general practitioner, who knew him well, sent him for an appointment to the hospital. The doctor who examined him said he could not find anything wrong, but the man insisted that he knew there was something, and that it was preventing him from doing his job. 'Oh, you're still working then?' said the doctor. He was surprised because he had taken the way the man had been dressed as an indication that he was not. 'Well, if you insist, I will ask for a second opinion.' The doctor did so and the dustman was found to have a hernia.

'First cast out the beam out of thine own eye; and then thou shalt see clearly to cast out the mote out of thy brother's eye.' This anecdote is not meant as a slander on the medical profession. But it does show that precisely what we base judgements on in any situation, medical, social or pastoral, is a lively question; and that the claim to professional status often pre-empts it. Any professional person needs to ask himself or herself what elements are involved in their case, and how they can use their expertise in a way which is answerable to the client rather than demeaning to them. But this begs a previous question, especially for clergy like myself, who grew up in an atmosphere of trust in professionalism and automatically assumed there were parallels between their own role and that of other professional helpers. The question is: are priests in any sense professionals, and what damage is done to their own potential ministry if, in a search for a greater definition to their own role and in emulation of other professions, they try to develop a professional persona rather than a religious one?

PROFESSIONALIZATION AND THE CHURCH'S MINISTRY

Professionalism as we now understand it is of relatively recent origin. It has gone hand-in-hand with the development of our society from a traditional base of small social units held together by ties of mutual obligation, deference, personally-vested authority and overarching beliefs, to a modern context characterized by a greater degree of interdependence (which has submerged or destroyed these smaller units), greater diversification of roles (within different spheres of life-work, leisure, industry, government, education, commerce and welfare), and greater use of rational systems of control and management rather than appeals to belief, custom, rights, duties and privileges. Our experience of life now is marked throughout by a division into relatively autonomous spheres, each of them – with the exception, perhaps, of leisure – more or less bureaucratically organized and led by teams of professionals. We are conscious, usually, of when we move from one sphere to another, and each of us is more familiar with some than others.

Religious belief no longer acts as a social cement for our society, as it did in the past when it cemented the majority, perhaps, but discriminated against minorities. It is now generally assumed that religious belief belongs to the private life of an individual, and its relevance to other spheres of life is disputed. If religion enters into these at all, then it is often in the shape of a problem (religious education in schools, communal politics, the law on abortion, Sunday trading, a cultural variable complicating the diagnosis of mental disease) rather than something contributing to a common sense of community and personal worth.

The effect on churches and the religious leadership within churches has been complicated. Because religious affiliation and church attendance is now much more a matter of choice than of birth and custom, most churches bear comparison with other forms of voluntary association based on shared interest, like clubs and societies. So, for example, one's status as a member is usually judged by how often one attends and one's degree of involvement; and the duties of the priest or minister as local church leader revolve increasingly around the maintenance of congregational life – visiting, encouraging new membership, anticipating problems.

As a profession, clergy no longer have the confidence to dispute the claims of other professionals, and feel they have lost ground to them. They tend to accept the assumption that the limits of their competence lie in the maintenance of church life and have little relevance to the other areas of life in which they and other members of the congregation may become involved. Within church life they have tended to become more and more *omni*competent, but if they venture outside it, their competence is at once disputed. They have become religious specialists *par excellence*, experts in whatever most affects church life – preaching, teaching, leading worship, outreach, recruitment and training – but with no role outside it.

This has had an effect on pastoral leadership, which has more and more come to mean sticking to one's own area of competence, i.e. church life, and not contesting the competence of those outside it. But there is one basic difficulty.

In the final analysis, one cannot typify religion as one sphere of life alongside others, since commitment to faith and the practice of belief is bound to affect all of life to a greater or lesser extent. Moreover, the real task of pastoring as an activity at once identified with the needs of the congregation but also orientating it to a goal beyond its own life in keeping pace with God's purposes for the world, has been obscured by the dominance of models for ministry drawn from notions of professional function, competence and control.

The overall effect of this dominance of professionalism has been to deter pastoral leaders from entering areas not directly connected with the maintenance of church life – areas where they feel they will be thought *in*competent – and to discourage congregations from coming into contact with the call to mission. It has made pastoring largely a matter of incorporating individuals as members of a congregation. It has increased the level of commitment demanded from the laity in terms of church allegiance and activity, without seriously challenging the position of the clergy as professionals. It has exaggerated the effectiveness of certain forms of activity, whilst completely ignoring others. It has encouraged certain voices to be heard while disenfranchising others, especially non-professional voices and voices which draw attention to the presence and call of religion outside the confines of church life.

A CONSPIRACY AGAINST THE LAITY

George Bernard Shaw said that all professions are conspiracies against the laity.[1] Certainly all professions limit the importance of the views of the 'clients' (whom they ostensibly serve) to determine how they respond in particular situations, in favour of the views of fellow professionals. They see their accountability in terms of adherence to common codes of practice rather than responsiveness to the views of those outside the profession, which they often denigrate as unrealistic or dangerous. They usually control their own training, recruitment and sources of information. They define for the client and for themselves the range of professional services they can provide, and usually resist attempts from outside to add to or subtract from these. Their response to any demand for radical change is to contain it by modifying their procedures, but without serious redistribution of powers or restructuring of the professional hierarchy. Thus it is a characteristic of professional bodies that they enlist help in the more mundane and less specialized aspects of their work by creating semi-professional categories, whose training and access to knowledge and status they still control.

The ways of professionals have always been defended in terms of the need to preserve the highest standards of service and personnel because of the importance of the jobs they do, which touch on matters of life and death and require trust and confidentiality. The clergyman's pastoral role can easily be defended in this way, though this is to ignore how any space for it at all is created by shared belief, and also the dimension of trust and mutual ministry which is supposed to characterize the Christian community as a whole.

Recently the behaviour of professional groups has come in for a good deal of criticism and analysis, in particular the tendency of professional bodies to invoke the highest moral principles to defend their own power within the institutions they are supposed to serve. For in example, the recent furore in the university world over the loss of security of tenure, academics saw this as a serious attack on academic freedom. But few of them attempted to explain how this freedom had been compromised among polytechnic lecturers who had never enjoyed it, or suggested that security of tenure should be extended to them. Among doctors, the same professional body which fought so hard to stay out of the National Health Service has fought strenuously against changes which will alter the balance of power within hospitals between doctors and groups of newer professionals. In so doing they have, rightly or wrongly, suggested that the whole principle of a social health service is at stake.

Clergy have not escaped this tendency. The present difficulties in the Church of England over the admission of women to the priesthood, the fear of some that it will invalidate their own ordination and the suggestion that the Church will change its character overnight from being a 'real' Church to a secularized sect are obviously connected. More directly, the development of various lay and ordained ministries has helped to supplement a numerically declining profession whose training and attitudes are constantly being challenged or made irrelevant by changing social circumstances. But the actual power these new ministers are allowed to exercise is always restricted, and arguably has led to a greater rather than less, clericalization of church structures. For not only has the distinction grown between nominal and committed church membership on the basis of involvement in 'church life', but also between ordinary and 'clericalized' laity, commissioned, trained and validated for particular tasks.

If anything, recent developments have restricted, rather than enhanced, the ability of some church denominations to respond to change. They have tended to emulate the management structures within other institutions, insisting on the need for more training and specialization, multiplying the number of professional grades, increasing the level of consultation; but without being able to apply the same techniques of assessment and accountability which keep other institutions responsive to changes within their own sphere.

THE OLDEST PROFESSION?

The word 'profession' has of course, two meanings; one religious and one secular. The religious meaning, indicating a profession of faith and the undertaking of vows to model one's life in accordance with that profession, is the more ancient, and is a call laid on all believers, not just those taking orders or monastic vows. So, for example, in the King James translation, the writer to the Hebrews addresses the whole Church in these words:

> Wherefore, holy brethren, partakers of the heavenly calling, consider the Apostle and High Priest of our profession, Christ Jesus. (3:1)

and again:

> Seeing that we have a great high priest that is passed

into the heavens, Jesus the Son of God, let us hold fast
to our profession. (4:14)

In these settings the word carries the meaning, elaborated
elsewhere in the epistle, that all followers of Christ accompany
one another, offer one another encouragement and are answerable to one another in a common pilgrimage towards a goal
which transcends our present state of existence – the New
Jerusalem.

Something of that excitement and sense of vocation has
carried over into the secular meaning of the word, as denoting
an occupation which requires great skill and commitment,
and is usually undertaken for the benefit of others. But this
also serves to hide the difference between the ends pursued
and the means of achieving them. The word 'professionalism',
a verbal coinage not noted until 1856, applies precisely to
that sense of identity shared by various secular professions,
incorporating a strong sense of identification between the individual and their role and accountability in performing it, but
limiting this form of self-consciousness to a distinct class of
people. In this form the idea of the professional works against
the whole notion of being the Church, and especially against
the notion of pastoring as an activity motivated by the sharing
of a common faith which encourages the whole community,
and not just individuals within it, in a ministry which goes
beyond the community itself.

The form pastoral action takes is bound to be personal,
voluntary and explorative. By making too close a comparison
with other professional forms of helping, we may ignore a
whole range of references to non-professional worlds like that
of the family, the neighbourhood, the voluntary association,
art and entertainment, with which the Church has long been
intimately associated and which remain important sources of
communal as well as individual identity. By so doing we may
also ignore or discount the informal patterns of caring and
service, the ministries of touch, of companionship, of sharing
in enthusiasms, of mutual enjoyment and laughter, which
characterize these worlds at their best.

Looking back to the world of George Herbert, it may be
that the link with that world had to be broken before the

Church could gain a sense of its own identity, distinct from the prevailing patterns of social authority and obligation. It may also be that the professionalization of the clergy and the development of church life have been a necessary stage in helping the Church to survive the break up of that traditional world, and to renew its mission in a more complicated and fragmented environment. But even within that world, the pastoral nature of the Church, and the parson's activity, pointed beyond immediate social arrangements to a fuller vision of human community. We need to pick up some of those themes again, and ask how the Church can be re-orientated once again towards a pastoral task which goes beyond the maintenance of its own church life. In the process the clergy may have to surrender their hard-won sense of professional identity in favour of a more open negotiation with the expectations of people inside and outside the Church. It may be that their professionalism is one of the major obstacles preventing a more responsive and mission-orientated ministry from the Church as a whole.

George Herbert's example may have a new relevance in all this. His life was a journey away from one source of authority and personal identity towards another, and this is reflected in his book. Underlying all the practical advice on behaviour and references to seventeenth-century village life, which now seem so distant, is Herbert's sense of calling to a source of authority and personal identity *apart* from anything which can be securely established in this narrow social world. The book is, at least in part, about how the pastor puts himself at the service of this power as its agent; and how this transforms the use he makes of the instruments of social authority which are his as a member of his class and profession. It seems to me that clergy need to renew such a quest today, this time discovering how it questions and transforms their sense of professional identity.

In his book, *The Clerical Profession*, Anthony Russell makes clear that the adoption of a professional identity by the clergy has never been entirely successful. What we may be seeing now, in the confusion which surrounds the clergy's role inside and outside the local church, is the final end of the attempt, by an appeal to the ideology of professionalism, to find a role in society which is generally recognized and non-controversial. In our society religion itself is a contested area, which is perceived as marginal to other spheres of activity, but which keeps trespassing on them. The ordained ministry will not find its pastoral heart until it accepts that religion itself is a source of controversy and that to be religious at all is to run the risk of losing identity rather than gaining it. What we termed in the last chapter the sense of the holy, which is non-rational, or perhaps better super-rational, is constantly breaking through and complicating the rational categories established by professionalism. For as Russell puts it:

Professionalization . . . [embraces] a considerable degree of rationalization . . . The degree to which rationaliz- ation, as a process by which more effective means might be designed to achieve known and empirical goals, can be applied to a profession the goals of which are at least in part supernatural, is limited.[2]

6

'HOW SHALL WE SING THE LORD'S SONG IN A STRANGE LAND?'

A FEW MONTHS AGO, a small group of us from the parish met to discuss worship. I had my own agenda for calling the meeting. Our parish is in a socially and racially mixed part of south London, and I was aware that for the black members of our church with memories of what church was like back home in countries like Trinidad, Guyana, Nigeria and Ghana, part of the difficulty in adjusting to conditions here was the difference in atmosphere in the churches. It was not just that they had not always felt welcomed, but that, in many cases, even where the liturgies were the same, much of what they felt belonged to the experience of real worship was missing in the churches here. So I wanted to find out what that missing element was by stirring individual memories of what church had been like back home. Perhaps we could regenerate something of the atmosphere in our own worship.

In the course of our discussion I realized that the situation was very much more complicated than I had imagined. Most people discussed the excitement of worship they remembered, the sense of occasion, the solemnity, the power of the singing, the length of the services, the contribution made by the different guilds and societies, and the respect given to figures with certain roles like the vicar, the organist and the president of the Mothers' Union; and they said how much they missed all this. But parallel to that another story emerged, of how oppressive the atmosphere had also been, how resistant to change, and how many of them had made up for the deficiencies in the life of their own churches by attending other churches and fellowships where there was a freer atmos-

phere and where popular traditions of music and celebration
were given more space. Their generation had already begun
to rebel and move away from the Christianity of their parents
which they felt was bound up with the social pattern established by colonialism. They had already begun to look back-
wards in pride to an African history before the coming of the
missionaries, and forwards to the rapid socio-economic and
political change happening not just in their own country, but
globally. Before they had even come to Britain, they were
already beginning to lose touch with the old world of which
church was a part.

What was being revealed was a very complex process of
cultural change in which the old world of their childhood was
disappearing for ever. The excitement of the worship they
remembered depended more on the fact that the whole community had been present, than on the beauty and appropriate-
ness of the liturgy or the preaching and personality of the
church leaders. They had been subconsciously aware of the
concentration in worship of the entire community, of seeing
their peers and elders transformed by their Sunday best and
various church robes and uniforms; moreover what had happened in and around worship formed part of the conversation
with their neighbours during the week.

At a crucial point in the discussion we realized that nostalgia for that sort of excitement was of no use to us in discussing
how we should be responsible for worship today, because the
particular social context in which we were called upon to
perform the ministry of worship was so different. The question
of how we could recreate something we remembered and
valued from the past no longer arose. On the other hand, how
we could pass on a spirit of worship to our children, how they
could catch it from us, became the vital question. In address-
ing this new question we all, black and white alike, became
fully aware that our children's experience of life, growing up
together in London now, was being formed by conditions
totally different from those we remembered ourselves. And in
ten years' time it would be different again. How could we
organize ourselves for that sort of change? Was it possible to
bring all these different worlds together at all?

Facing the question involved taking fully into account the

changes in culture which are happening all the time. The word 'culture' is a tricky one. As many people have pointed out, it is often used as a code word for other differences of race or class which we are afraid to face directly. In certain sorts of discussion phrases like 'the black experience' or 'working class culture' are treated as if they denote cultural entities which never change and never mingle. But looking from another vantage point, as we did in the course of discussion, or as might happen in discussing pop music, for example, or analysing the appeal of advertisements, we are made aware of different sets of contrasts and continuities in our experience.

It soon became evident that there were strong parallels in the experience of all of us who could remember a church childhood, that we were all saying goodbye to a set of social and cultural conditions that had created atmospheres which could not be reproduced in exactly the same way again. For example, the influence that musical and liturgical forms developed in cathedral worship had on the worship of most parish churches even fifteen years ago, was a sort of colonialism, if you like, based on the very best traditions provided by 'high' culture in the narrow sense of the term. Go into a church built even twenty-five years ago and you will find that the furnishings assume a style of worship which has since been considerably changed and fragmented. We all feel a nostalgia for something which has been altered for ever by the growing impact of various forms of popular culture. 'O show me the way back, the long way back to childhood.' But, of course, the way back no longer exists.

As well as people like myself who could be called 'exiles', there were also at the meeting individuals who could be called 'searchers'. These were people with no childhood links with the church. When we asked one person about childhood experiences that he could now name as religious he could not remember one definite incident. What had brought him into contact with the church as a teenager was the feeling of searching for something, though he did not know what it was. It is hard for those of us who are exiles to put ourselves into the shoes of someone who has had no impetus from their past or background, no framework in which they can recognize and name experiences as 'religious' or God-given.

It is very hard for those who have been guided by a generalized sense of belief since they were children, who have not had to go out of their way to find belief, to understand the situation of someone whose faith has been formed by following hints and guesses and a process of trial and error. But increasingly this experience of individual search is the rule rather than the exception. Even those who are coming forward for ministry in the churches may be people who have only been Christians in a particular denomination for a few years. Often they have a very interesting history behind them of search inside and outside the churches, of false dawns and fresh starts. Often they have powerful experiences to tell. They will have been largely responsible for their own direction, picking up information where they can, trying different philosophies and ways of prayer and combining them, considering and choosing between alternatives. Their stories of search do not have a lot in common with each other, let alone with the experience of those brought up in a faith. Yet there is a long tradition, including accounts like Augustine's *Confessions* and Bunyan's *Pilgrim's Progress*, which points to how essential these accounts of personal search are for all of us – searchers and exiles alike.

NURTURE

How do we help people to grow in a congregation when there is such a diversity of experience? How do seekers and exiles coexist in the same congregation? The religious and cultural memories of individuals in an inner-city congregation like ours are so diverse. If they are awakened, will the effect be to divide people rather than bring them together? On the other hand, if we ignore them and try to impose something in their place, are we not then acting unpastorally, by treating people at less than their full value, which includes the memories and experiences they bring with them? It is a very real problem, because as soon as things begin to change in a church, it revives memories of what was possible in the past, which may have the effect again of valuing one set of individuals' experiences at the expense of another.

Faced with the reality of cultural diversity, some proponents of church growth assert that it is impossible for the gospel to be effectively communicated if a congregation is so mixed that you cannot appeal to a common stock of images, experiences and memories. A culturally diverse congregation will not attract new members as fast as one which focuses on the fears, needs and hopes of a particular group. Targeting a particular group may possibly be the only way forward for a large city centre church; but for a local church and a local ministry struggling with the challenge to relate in a positive way to a local area and the variety of communities and individuals represented there, and with a history behind it of that sort of involvement, this sort of advice feels like an admission of failure.

This is the challenge presented to the very idea of a local church. The level at which we are called to ministry as the people of God, is precisely the level in which there has been most strain and fragmentation in our society. This is what the wealth of information brought together in the *Faith in the City* report revealed most clearly. People living in many urban areas suffer not only from bad pay, bad housing and an insufficient, badly provided range of services. They suffer also from the damage done to local networks by the impact of rapid social and economic change imposed on them as the by-product of decisions taken elsewhere. The reason why the report caused such controversy was that it drew attention to the cost, in terms of the real pain experienced in the lives of many individuals, brought about by this process. The widening of the gap between the haves and the have-nots; the fuelling of tension between different groups as a result of increased competition for a reduced level of employment and provision of social housing and other social benefits; the crisis in the management and provision of local services brought about in many areas by the fierce political struggle for control between local and national government; all these factors have played a part in damaging people's feelings of pride in themselves and their community, of their sense of identity and of responsibility for each other. All local institutions, whether schools, churches, youth organizations, tenants' and residents' associations, health practices, have felt the effects. Paradoxically, there is often most talk of community where there is least sense of it, and even those who have benefited most from the changes are also often aware of something having been lost in the process.

Is it true, given the diversity and fragmentation of our society today, that there is indeed 'no such thing as society', just a series of institutional arrangements and controls to enable families and individuals to co-exist? Or are churches, by their own life and witness, still pointers to deeper sources for community, care and responsibility? The struggle to maintain and develop local ministry is an attempt to answer that question in the affirmative. It is a risky enterprise because it can easily become trapped by cynicism and frustration on the one hand – a feeling of why bother at all? – or nostalgia for old patterns of community that can never be recreated anyway (except in a 'heritage' exhibition!), and which often emphasize a sense of alienation rather than overcome it. Nevertheless, I believe that local pastoral ministry can release positive energy for the growth of community, outside as well as inside the congregation, as long as real attention is given to what sources are actually available, not our fantasies about them.

This often involves us in making the transition from one meaning of the word 'culture' to another. As well as describing a state of affairs which is already the case and which one inherits automatically, 'culture' can also describe an experience or state of being which one can help to create. This is the way teachers use the term, for example, when they talk of 'classroom culture' as the means of providing the right conditions to facilitate learning. Culture in this sense refers to the largely invisible sources of psychological support and undergirding provided by commonly-held beliefs, assumptions and ideals, without which visible institutions and enterprises cannot be sustained.

Another example of this use of the term is the present discussion about Eastern Europe and the Soviet Union after the demise of communism. This has focused on differences in political cultures. It asks such questions as: is there enough material in terms of shared memories, an underground culture of resistance, and renewed hope, to create a democratic future for these countries? Or are they too traumatized by Marxism and too trapped by bad history? How do people learn to be free? What local institutions still exist to help this process? The questions confronted in areas of urban deprivation in this country are not so different, though local institutions have not so much been made the object of direct attack, as shouldered aside.

Other examples of this usage abound. It has become popular because it recognizes that so many of the old sources of community support and identity have fragmented and disappeared that a more self-conscious attempt is needed to create culture in various ways. So people speak of 'enterprise culture', 'company culture', or 'media culture', and so on and so on. In each case the word 'culture' focuses on the level of hidden and less formal interaction and sharing of values behind what is openly expressed in ideologies, systems of government, legal or religious institutions.

It could be argued that no vision of society is possible without the existence of these hidden substrata, and that religious faith has a vital role in informing them. It is no accident that in many totalitarian countries, religious faith has become a vehicle of resistance. The crucial question, which often confronts us in different ways, is how we create a sense of belonging which at the same time acknowledges and facilitates the process of change rather than denying it. Culture can be seen as a static quality belonging to different people, religions, races and groups, or as something dynamic, a by-product of collaborative human effort, and, as such, *constantly* changing.

One might say that the point we reached in our parish discussion, involved a transition from one sense of the word to the other. Instead of asking ourselves how we could reproduce elements of separate cultures in an altered context, we began to ask how we could together create a healthy culture in our church which included the new experiences of our children and the seekers among us, as well as our own memories.

CHILDREN IN THE WAY

Another report in the Church of England which has had an impact far beyond its immediate subject is *Children in the Way*.[1]

Though a much smaller report than *Faith in the City* it was based on an equally wide range of research among actual congregations. This brought into focus, as the basic datum, the huge diversity in congregational size and churchmanship, the resources available within and outside different congregations, the types of people they involved, their relationship with other local groups and institutions like the family, the school, recreational facilities, Scouts and Guides and their differing contributions to local culture. This diversity made it clear from the start that any approach which tried to standardize methods of dealing with children in church was bound to fail.

To be confronted with the pastoral task of reaching children is immediately to become aware that there is a problem of barriers created by differences in culture and understanding. In dealing with children we become instinctively adaptionist. We have to take account of their expectations and ways of perceiving things if we are going to communicate at all. This makes a good introduction to other situations where we cannot assume common expectations, perceptions and cultural norms.

Because of this diversity of culture and context, the report understood that, if goals were to be set for the Church's action among children, then it had to be in terms of sharing common aims and beliefs about children and their significance for the whole Church, rather than common training programmes and methods of teaching.

The report was unusual in combining expert opinion and children's actual experience, which was portrayed not as some timeless quality belonging to an age of innocence, but something which is as radically altered by new social and economic conditions as that of adults. Children cannot be treated as people without a story to tell, or a story that we know about already, on the assumption that, after all, we have all been children once ourselves. The report suggested that space should be made for children's stories and ways of being present in every aspect of church life and worship, not just Sunday school. How this could be done would depend very much on local circumstances, so the report confined itself to providing examples of successful contact rather than overall strategies.

It argued that if space was made for children in this way, then there was the real possibility that they could give something for the whole community to share, and that their story would become related to the story of the whole church community. Thus the report moved away from a discussion of the particular problems of children in church to the need for a form of address to, and education of, all believers, based on a sense of common pilgrimage.

Children often expose the limitations of adult forms of behaviour, in the hurt they sustain because of adults' carelessness; in their unwillingness to restrict their demands to what we consider reasonable; and in their failure to be impressed by what we regard as important. As in the fairy tale, it is the child amongst us who often points out that the Emperor has no clothes. Listening to someone's story is such a basic act, and so much of our life together depends on it, that we take it for granted. No good parent, no good lover or neighbour, would think of not listening to the other's story. Yet how much pastoral activity among children stands up to this test? If it is true that we do not listen to children, what other voices in the Church may we also be ignoring?

Pastoral care is a form of communication as well as of assistance. The oddest people are able to communicate with children – clowns and old people as well as experts in child behaviour – and children pick up information in odd ways. If you want to communicate with a child, you take account of their story, and communicating your values to them often involves you in telling your own. How much professionalism is really necessary in this form of communication, which actually constitutes so much of our care for each other? Other qualifications, more generally available, such as sensitivity, compassion, attention and respect are equally important. They need to be present in the professional role as well. Indeed, in one sense, the only difference between professional and non-professional caring is that the professional should be relied on to deliver this form of attention to a wider circle of people than just immediate friends and neighbours and to act even when his or her affections are not in this way immediately engaged. This involves a particular form of self-discipline, one that is required of all those who share a Christian sense of vocation, not just selected orders of the lay and ordained.

COMMUNITY DEVELOPMENT AND COMMUNITY WORK

A church interacts with its local environment in different ways, through its ordained representatives, its relation to community networks, the organization of its worship and the messages transmitted by particular pastoral policies (over baptism, for example) and the pastoral care of individuals. The cultural milieux in which pastoral care is exercised are always as important as the form the care takes. Changes in milieux have the effect of also altering the impact of different kinds of pastoral activity. Marriage instruction is just one example of this. The impact of the same marriage discipline and teaching about it in an area where there is a high proportion of people living singly, with or without children, is bound to be different from that in an area where the vast majority are living as couples in their own homes.

For a pastoral ministry such as that exercised in the Church of England, the basic problem has been how a ministry rooted in a common form of society which has gone forever, can adapt to the flux, fragmentation and increasingly diverse cultural context of today. Professionalism among the clergy and laity is one answer which focuses on what we can do as providers, and looks for ways of standardizing levels and types of caring and the training given for them. But arguably the very diversity of the contexts in which we live and carry out our calling is now so great that such an approach has become increasingly counter-productive; it provides the wrong model of standardization and control.

As I mentioned at the outset of this book, one of the peculiarities of the modern context is that so many of the factors that go into the making of our experience seem outside our control. The fact of cultural diversity is just one of them. Before we can approach questions of what we should *do* in the context of cultural diversity (e.g., How can we bring people together?) we should first examine our fears about it and learn to live with it. Being comes before doing. We cannot become truly responsive to a particular situation until we have recognized it as our own. We are all part of the same wilderness. This is the source of some of our greatest threats and fears, and unless we face it ourselves we are unable to help others.

The relevance of this statement becomes more obvious as we examine the different levels of ministry suggested by the terms 'community development' and 'community'. First, community work:

> Community work is the enabling or empowering process of face-to-face work, with, rather than for, groups of local people who have identified their needs and wish to work collectively to do something about it. If it is about enabling people collectively to do things for themselves, that is not only a crucial intervention, but one that is complex, demanding and requiring the highest standards in skills and personal qualities.[2]

This statement from the Church of England's Board of Social Responsibility's report *Church and Community Work* gives a very clear picture of the thinking behind a lot of community work. It is about empowerment and involvement of local people. It requires face-to-face interaction between a professional worker and local people, through which they make their wishes known and the worker makes professional skills available to them so that together they do something about it. Usually this is in the context of setting up and running a project which after a few years, if the worker's job has been done properly, can then be left to the local people to run themselves.

There are many parallels between this sort of activity and local pastoral ministry at its best. It is purposive but also collaborative and personal. It avoids the danger of de-skilling people through professional intervention by making their wishes and involvement crucial at every stage and aiming consistently for their empowerment. But as our experience of this sort of work grows, its limitations also become clearer.

First, as the statement shows, it places a very heavy burden of expectation on the individual worker. He or she needs 'the highest standards in skills and personal qualities'. Often the job description actually involves the worker in defining a particular project as well as helping it to come into being. This puts the pressure on the worker to set it up as quickly as possible, since the funding for the job is usually limited to a few years and the pressure is on to have something to show the management committee. Quite often strain develops because of the levels of expectation involved on all sides and the inevitable disappointments.

Secondly, the 'groups of local people' mentioned in the statement are not necessarily representative of the whole community in which they live. Any group which has already defined its needs and is prepared to do something about them is likely to be self-selecting. Furthermore, what characterizes a lot of 'deprived areas' is a *lack* of community. This has two effects. Sometimes a group of local people will become highly committed and energized, but this energy and commitment fails to spread and the rest of the community never 'owns' a project in spite of the joint efforts of the worker and the group. At other times there is the danger that the project may be taken over by a group of people who claim to speak for the whole community but are actually self-interested rather than having its needs truly at heart. More attention needs to be given to the concept of 'empowerment'. Sometimes to empower one set of people is to put another group of people at a disadvantage.

Thirdly, the sort of structure demanded by this model of working often militates against what it is trying to do. The employment of a community worker assumes a body of people able to provide the worker with a proper job description, proper terms of pay and conditions, and a proper committee structure to manage and assess his or her work. In many areas this all belongs to professional rather than local culture (though local churches, clubs and associations have some resources for it within their experience of managing their own affairs). In many community initiatives the various elements necessary to create proper conditions to employ a worker occur at the end of the process rather than at the beginning, which puts even more strain on the worker's role. Often several stages of development need to have happened first before this way of working can be successfully implemented.

Finally, for all the reasons already mentioned, it is often difficult for a community worker to leave at the time his or her contract is supposed to finish, either because a project has hardly begun to get off the ground, or because in spite of the best efforts of all concerned, a degree of mutual dependence has been created which is difficult to break. In the quest for further funding from outside agencies, the participants experience a loss of control over their own project as they try to fit the various criteria qualifying it for support from the different agencies.

Several questions need first to be asked before community work of the sort we have described (i.e. sponsored, managed and directed locally rather than by an outside agency) can begin. What will be the possible impact of the new initiative on existing social networks? How might it be affected by the tensions that already exist in the community? How can local knowledge and ways of coping be affirmed and incorporated into the structure of the project? What new sources of energy and commitment may be available in the wider community? One has to live with the problem before finding the solution. In this sense community development is a necessary precondition for many forms of community work.

David Thomas, Director of the Community Development Foundation, gave the following definition of community development in a paper presented at the London Diocesan Board for Social Responsibility in 1987:

> In community development the community is not seen as a static context in which individual groups operate, but . . . as a live, social system in its own right. The purpose of community work is to develop the functioning and effectiveness of particular groups. The purpose of community development is to develop the functioning and effectiveness of a whole community. It is about the competence of a defined community to respond to a range of problems that are generated internally – e.g., a conflict between black and white, between young and old; and to a range of threats and challenges issued to the community by those outside – e.g., by governments, by big business, or even by natural causes such as disasters . . .

Nowhere is that more urgent than in poor urban areas where individual skills and energy, resources and self-confidence have been eroded – not just by the struggle for survival, but by the indifference of government and many professions.[3]

Within the terms of this statement the 'defined community' may be as small as a local church or as big as a neighbourhood. What it does is draw attention in a different way to the three factors we have already touched on in discussing the sharing of memories, hopes and purposes across the barrier of different cultures – young and old, black and white, popular and high-brow. These are 1) the dynamism of different cultures, i.e., the fact that they are always changing and interacting; 2) their nature as vehicles of potential conflict and resistance; and 3) the fact that they may be created willingly as well as inherited inevitably.

To fulfil its ministry the local church is not always involved in community work, but community development *is* a necessary corollary of mission, because our very nature as *ecclesia*, people called together by God to serve his purposes in the world, entails the search for greater unity and community (see the opening chapters of the Letter to the Ephesians). 'By their fruits ye shall know them.' The local church may be many things in relation to its immediate area. Sometimes what it is, is at odds with what it claims to do. The tensions present in the life of the area often present themselves as problems within the life of the congregation itself in worship, ministry and . mission. The local church, therefore, may become either a focus for resistance to change among individuals or groups, or itself a sign that change can be negotiated and a new sense of belonging together created by tapping into new and old sources of energy and survival.

This ministry is necessary for another reason also. The very fact that churches live their corporate life so much on the margins of modern society rather than at its centre, means that sometimes they have a better entrée into the invisible networks of memory, belief and feeling than institutions and agencies more centrally placed. That makes them particularly well placed to reflect and embody the task of community development. The case has yet to be proved that a way of organizing society which banishes a sense of the holy to the outskirts of its ways is any better at bringing down the barriers between people than one which respects it. As the complexities of the Rushdie affair have shown, the liberal agnosticism entrenched in the culture of the majority has its own areas of blindness and insensitivity. In modern society, religious belief may be a source of even greater division and bitterness, or it may be the joker in the pack which transcends apparently insurmountable barriers of race, class and culture – even creed.

It is this which gives the special flavour, challenge and sense of urgency to the pastoral task today. For as a development worker in the London Diocese, Ann Morisy, has written:

> In the context of community ministry, pastoral care is not a static repetitious response of the local church to the well-being of parishioners but becomes a point of discernment, a research tool, and a prompt for a purposeful, corporate, response.[4]

There is a spirituality which goes with this response – one of intercession. Churches should be places of beseeching, where there is a sense of the incompleteness of all human community without God, and a constant moving to and fro between the two in thought, prayer and action. Nowhere is this more necessary than in the wilderness where it is easy to wander from the right track without realizing it, and what seems to be ahead of us often turns out to be a mirage. In the Bible the ministry of people like Abraham, Moses and Jesus himself consisted in standing in the gap between the purposes of God and our general failure to meet them.

To be pastorally active as a church is not in opposition to the call to be contemplative. In fact intercessory prayer brings the two together, because it is both the product of active concern for the community and a waiting on God. It is both a way of being and a way of doing. Churches are on the fringes of many different worlds and make contact with them in many different ways. Instead of talking about this negatively as marginalization, which brings with it the temptation to use 'community work' as a way of getting back into the centre, we may use it as a place where we experience our relative powerlessness but also where we find vision.

In intercession we often bring before God the pain of another's situation and our relative powerlessness to help them. We search in our spirit for the ways in which God may nevertheless be present or able to act, and in the course of our reflection our own hope for them and for ourselves is revived. Out of this often comes the gifts we need to be servants in these situations ourselves – above all, patience, discernment, imaginative sympathy, and a willingness not to rest content with the way things are but to struggle for something better.

7

BODY LANGUAGE AND OTHER
METAPHORS

IN THE LITURGIES we use, the sermons we hear and the church literature we read, we have become used to the dominance of 'the Body' as *the* metaphor for the Church. But the fluid nature of the circumstances in which the local church is called to minister today calls for a readjustment of this metaphor of the Church and a search for others which help us to look outwards for a sense of community as well as inwards at the internal life of a congregation. For the following reason.

Body language is particularly susceptible to being used to justify institutional arrangements and the functions of individuals within them. In its original contexts in Paul's letters it refers primarily to the relationship between the earthly church and its heavenly origin and head, the exalted Christ (see for example Colossians 1:15–20; Ephesians 4:15–16). But in practice we use it more as a metaphor for different ministries within the Church and the need for them to work together (see Ephesians 4 as a whole, and 1 Corinthians 12). Thus the metaphor can easily come to be used to vindicate the life of the Church as a thing in itself, self-justifying and complete, to which all forms of ministry are directed as a means of maintaining its existence. If then a further equation is made between the full life of the Church as informed by the Spirit of Christ and the church life and activity visible in congregations, the metaphor helps to keep things as they are rather than suggest developments which would cause a certain amount of conflict and dislocation.

Other metaphors therefore need to be brought into play, which emphasize the nature of the Church as a *project* – that is, a plan, scheme or purpose thrown into our world by God which requires our co-operation in its execution. At the centre of the Church's life is the initiative of God revealed in the incarnation of Jesus Christ and the redemption of the world wrought through him. The Church has no existence, and in that sense no body, outside the particular part it has to play in the economy of salvation for which it still waits on God for total completion.

> For he has made known to us in all wisdom and insight the mystery of his will, according to his purpose which he set forth in Christ as a plan for the fullness of time, to unite all things in him, things in heaven and things on earth. (Ephesians 1: 9–10 RSV)

It is important, therefore, to make room for metaphors like that of the servant and messenger, or pilgrimage, as expressive of the life of the Church. Then it becomes possible to use traditional terms for ministry, like apostle, evangelist, prophet, pastor and teacher, less as titles defining function within the Church and more as terms which express the different ways in which we experience the presence and love of God – through the preaching of good news, or the exercise of care, or the challenge to a false sense of security. All these activities flow into one another. All of them change according to the particular context in which they are exercised.

This opens the way to a more dynamic view of the Church's ministry as a whole, as being directed beyond its own life towards the true worship of God at all times and in all places. All the terms for ministry are connected with one another as ways of discerning the presence and activity of the Spirit of God. Therefore it is possible, in returning to the theme of pastoring, to see it as having as much reference to the dynamic nature of the Church as other aspects of ministry, like evangelism or prophecy.

The following pages suggest how some new and old images and metaphors, when applied to the ordained ministry, may be used in practice to support a dynamic view of the local church as an agent of change as well as stability, struggle as well as security, vision as well as remembrance. They are not meant to apply exclusively to the ordained, but their acceptance by the ordained may in certain circumstances facilitate a 'revisioning' by the whole church community. Some of them apply only loosely to the ordained. But the willingness to entertain them is perhaps one way of escaping the strait-jacket of professional terminology whilst keeping in touch with the changing elements of a persona which is often projected on to clergy and over which they have no real control.

THE STRANGER IN YOUR MIDST

There is a phrase in the Bishop's charge to priests at their ordination which intrigues me for the way it takes common (though now ancient) images and gives them new meaning – as Jesus did when he coined the phrase 'fishers of men': 'You are to be messengers, watchmen and stewards of the Lord.'

'Messenger' carries with it the connotation of someone who is sent, in other words, an apostle; but also the sense of someone coming to a particular community with something (a message) from outside. These two roles of apostleship and outsider are closely related, especially when examined in the light of St Paul's account of his own ministry among people of different cultures, contained in his letters. For whether Paul is among the Jewish Christians in Jerusalem, or among Gentile Christians in places like Corinth, he remains to some extent the outsider, and therefore the one who is seen as likely to upset the status quo wherever he arrives.

Paul himself sees this role as being derived directly from the message with which he has been entrusted: that God, through the death and resurrection of Christ, has broken down the barrier between Gentiles and Jews, slaves and free persons, male and female. In other words, the old ways of making community, for setting boundaries to community and defining insiders from outsiders, have been overthrown. In their place God has set forward a universal vision of community, of which the Church – those called into community with Christ – is meant to be a sign and a servant.

So in any situation where a particular church attempts to

define the limits of community too narrowly, re-erecting old barriers, or establishing new ones, Paul stands against it. He sees this as an intrinsic part of his apostleship. So, for example, in Galatians he rebukes Peter for betraying his ministry as an apostle, when in response to Jewish Christian pressure Peter stops eating with Gentile Christians in Antioch (Galatians 2). On the other hand, in speaking to a mixed community in Rome, Paul is careful to preserve the rights of conscience of Jewish Christians who will not eat meat which is not kosher (Romans 14).

His ministry, therefore, is full of paradox. In any situation he is likely to support the position of those in danger of being excluded, as outsiders, from full fellowship, even though he may not see things quite as they do. He becomes a Jew to win Jews, and a Gentile to win Gentiles, thereby demonstrating his willingness to identify himself with whichever community he has been sent to. But at the same time, as a Jew who behaves like a Gentile in the sight of Jews, and as the 'Jewish' opponent of Gentile 'immorality', he constantly runs the risk of exclusion himself. Because he sees himself as being entrusted with a ministry which includes a vision of community wider than anything yet fully established, Paul remains to some extent an outsider in every situation. This makes him vulnerable to criticism, but at the same time, preserves his freedom as a minister.

The arrangements made for ministry today in most denominations mean that ordained ministers still usually come to the local congregation from outside. This bare fact puts them in a very powerful, but at the same time ambivalent position. The shape their ministry will take within a congregation depends a lot on what signals they give when they first arrive. Will they act immediately to establish their own status, attacking or placating those they see as the strongest threat to that status? Will they endorse the status quo as they find it, or act immediately to overturn it?

Paul's own example is very informative about the creative use the ordained outsider can make of his or her own role on first arriving in a congregation, especially where there are strong tensions within the church and the local area. In situations of pastoral conflict, usually associated with certain groups' inability to free themselves sufficiently from their Jewish or Gentile past, Paul often stood for a wider vision of the people of God as against the narrower vision of those who currently had the power to determine opinion and membership within a local congregation. In doing so, he identified himself with those outside the congregation as firmly as with those within it.

Ordained ministers need to be aware of their ability to act as advocates for those vulnerable to definition as outsiders. They are themselves in a powerful but still vulnerable position when they first come to a congregation. They have been sent from outside as someone with authority. In some church situations, they can be the one outsider an existing congregation is obliged to allow inside. Many congregations, especially if they are small, have very powerful informal means, often used only semi-consciously, of making some people welcome and keeping others at a distance. The formal authority of ordained ministers makes it impossible for them to be excluded, and usually when they arrive a sincere attempt is made to welcome them. But often there is an unspoken question behind these initial approaches: 'Is he, or she, one of us?'

This will often be expressed in very positive terms: 'We've always been a very friendly congregation.' 'We don't seem to have the same troubles as you find in other churches.' 'We've always been a church for families.' 'We like people who are prepared to roll up their sleeves and get stuck in.' 'We've always prided ourselves on the beauty of the worship here.' But each of these statements is an attempt to define the situation in a particular way. Each of them therefore prompts a question. Who would be regarded as unfriendly or troublesome? Who are regarded as fitting the category of 'families', bearing in mind that the number of people living as two parents and two children in their own home is vastly outnumbered in many areas (not just the inner city) by people living together or singly in different ways? What is considered as pulling one's weight in the congregation and how does it relate to prayer and mission? Who finds the atmosphere of the worship constricting and oppressive and why? It is important for someone, whose voice can be heard, to maintain enough freedom to ask these questions. It does not have to be the ordained minister. But in situations where open conflict has been discouraged, theirs may be the only outsider's voice powerful enough to make itself heard.

In these situations, it is important that new ministers, in their eagerness to get themselves established, do not act in a way which would reaffirm the way things are. But to challenge it, does not mean that one has act confrontationally. Clergy arrive in a situation bringing their own baggage of hopes, fears and disappointments. They can easily project their own worst fears on to individuals before they have any sense of what is really going on. Many ministries are damaged from the start because the projection and counter-projection that goes on between the ordained minister and members of the congregation makes it impossible for real communication to begin. Paul often settled in an area first, supporting himself by practising his trade, and getting to know the town and its varieties of religion, before he began ministry in earnest. Being present without fully belonging, and being aware of how that affects different people, is as useful a role as any for a newly-arrived minister to play at the beginning.

The seeds of change are usually contained within a situation. When a new minister arrives, there is the feeling that everyone can make a new start. Old bits of history which people would rather forget can be decently buried before they begin to affect the relationship with the newcomer. Voices which previously went unheard in the congregation have an opportunity to make themselves heard. Because the new minister does not as yet belong to anyone in particular, there is the possibility for people to change places. Some people may be glad to be released from a role with which they have become increasingly uncomfortable. Some may find it impossible to make the adjustment to working with someone new. Others who previously had stayed very much on the periphery of a congregation, or had been forced outside, may want to come back into it again.

As well as the open life of the community, there is a hidden life which contains its greatest fears and hopes. The opportunity has to be given for this hidden life to reveal itself gradually to all concerned. By acting too quickly to impose a new structure, or establish formal leadership in a congregation, instead of freeing a situation, a new minister can actually create a new form of oppressive control. In the worst scenarios, the minister can be engaged in bitter conflict with powerful individuals while the rest of the congregation look on. Often this conflict is fed, on the one hand, by the minister's own need to be in control and, on the other hand, by the fear of change focused by the minister's arrival. Paul's example of apostolic leadership suggests that the ordained minister is often most useful to the life of a congregation when he or she is prepared to stay on the edge of it. The periphery is the place where hidden tensions become visible and growth is made possible.

THE BEARER OF THE MEANINGS OF OTHERS

In traditional society, the parson was not just a significant figure in the local hierarchy, but one bearing communal expectations about what it meant to be a Christian. The word 'parson' is actually derived from the Middle English spelling for 'person'. As Herbert's *A Priest to the Temple* shows, the analogies used of a parson's role contained a much richer range of reference than the merely authoritarian and hierarchical. Some of these analogies point to conflict and tension rather than reconciliation or satisfaction with the present state of things.

It is important today to reflect on the range of unofficial images and analogies an ordained person's presence and activity evokes among the people they work with as well as the ones currently endorsed by their training and the 'invisible audience' of fellow professionals. Many of these images and expectations are confused and mutually contradictory. But being willing to communicate with individuals and groups of people on this level is part of what constitutes the cost of ministry. As Herbert recognized, one cannot receive love for and affirmation of one's role without accepting the possibility of hate for it and rejection as well.

Furthermore, the ability of ordained ministers to control these good and bad responses to their role and to be protected from their effects on how they see themselves and their work, is strictly limited in contrast to many professions. This is because the minister's role originates in the profession of faith – their own and that of the church as a whole. In these circumstances there can be no strict distinction between the person and the role and no path for the performance of it except identification and responsibility. The word 'responsibility' already implies bearing the weight of other people's hopes and expectations. 'Answerability' is another word to describe it, but one which also includes to a greater degree the sense of being answerable to God as well as to other people for what one does – something always intimately associated with leadership in the biblical witness.

Most people experience entering into such a role for others as a loss of control over their own personality and behaviour. But one way of understanding it, as also the importance of *staying in* the role, is the modern analogy of group therapy. The presence of someone set aside and recognized by the group as a therapist immediately alters the context in which members of the group communicate with each other. In the performance of their role for the group, the therapist's silence and non-intervention is as important as their occasional questions and reflections which are deliberately open-ended to facilitate further communication in the group.

It is better therefore in these circumstances to call the therapist the *bearer* rather than the *agent* of change. Change occurs less by the therapist's direct intervention than by the significance their silence carries for members in the group. The presence of the therapist as a significant outsider, not fully belonging to the group or any section of it, helps to mirror back to individuals their own hidden anxieties, fears and hopes of recognition. The therapist becomes the object of appeals for support, questioning and animosity. In this way the potential for conflict present in the group, which is the source of much hidden fear and tension within it but also the possibility of change for the better, is brought into the open. This increases the interaction between other members of the group rather than diminishing it, and allows things to come to light which have impeded it in the past.

Who is the agent of change in this situation? Not the outsider, though the outsider's presence and willingness to play the role, assists it. The agent of change is the group itself. Perhaps this example, as well as providing an analogy for pastoral practice within the local congregation, provides a metaphor also for the theological status of an ordained ministry among the *laos*, the connection between the ordained priesthood and the priesthood of all believers? For as bearers of meaning for others and as agents responsible under the grace of God for our own change, we are all priests.

The analogy between the ordained minister and the group therapist is not accidental. In both cases their power is seen initially as derived from sources outside the group – the therapist's professional training for example, and knowledge of past cases. In the course of therapy individuals become more aware that the power comes as much from within the group as from outside it, and aware of the significance they can carry for each other. At this point the therapist can become more free to intervene directly as a member of the group and leave behind the role, or succession of roles, assigned to them in the process by various individuals or by the group as a whole. Paradoxically, the therapist's power, which actually derives from their bestowed status within the group more than from their professional training, *diminishes* in inverse proportion as their personal freedom increases.

Wesley Carr suggests that the representative nature of ordained ministry allows the minister to learn a lot about the inner life of a congregation through the various projections that are made on to him or her. Some of these projections will be friendly, or flattering, some of them will be hostile, because there is no growth without both dependency and conflict. In the course of getting to know a congregation, ministers will have to accept the roles assigned to them before real communication can begin and they can more clearly define what is to be their particular task for that congregation. This does not exclude them, however, from disappointing some expectations and encouraging others. They are not under the control of group expectations in the performance of their role because they are simultaneously aware of having been put there for a purpose which extends beyond the life of the congregation as they find it, especially to those who remain outside it. But without this willingness to negotiate roles, there is just 'one person's fantasies about himself, and a set of images held by others'.[1]

Some people would argue that the professional identity of ordained ministry, predominantly white, male and middle-class, is too strong for it ever to act in this facilitative way. In their view, it is impossible for the clergy to act in ways which do anything other than establish the status quo in ever more subtle ways. Until there is a ministerial priesthood in churches which truly reflects the churches' present member-ship in terms of class, race and gender, there is no hope for a pastoral leadership which can act other than to reinforce its own status

But the status of the ordained minister, as the analogy drawn from group therapy shows, is much more ambiguous than it appears at first. It is as much assigned by others as it is self-maintained. The whole notion of being called to a mutual ministry in the Body of Christ encompasses the idea that we can enter into the situation and travail of others, and they are able to enter into ours. A lot depends on how we use the status we have been assigned; whether we can live with its ambivalence, the hostility it generates as well as respect, or whether we act defensively, always in the interests of reduc-ing the level of strain to our professional identity.

THE WATCHER

The Bible contains some arresting images which emphasize the importance of a task of care and leadership conducted at the edge of a community rather than at its centre. The nomad is one image. Another is the watchman who stands on the city wall and looks out to see what is coming. His role is particularly important in times of crisis. How quick he is to spot a danger may determine the safety of a city. On the other hand, he is usually the first person to bring the good news of its relief or liberation. It is not surprising therefore that the image is often associated with the task of prophecy, as in Ezekiel 33:7: 'So you, son of man, I have made a watchman for the house of Israel; whenever you hear a word from my mouth, you shall give them warning from me' (RSV).

In my mind this image has become connected with that of the modern porter, receptionist, or commissionaire, all people who are designated to stand between the institution they serve and the world outside. They are also people who carry messages between departments, observe who comes in and goes out and often have a strong understanding of what is happening underneath the surface. They are the bridges between the informal life of the institution as a community of people and its open life as an organization. As people on the edge of an institution they may have special insight into the way it works. They are therefore most aware of the gap which exists between what the institution claims about itself and what is actually the case, partly because – like the prophet – they have little power over it in a formal sense.

Insight, prophecy, vision – a community lives by these things as much as it does by the effectiveness of its organizations and the efficiency with which it carries out its different functions. Ordained ministers, as people who belong to the outside as well as the inside of a local congregation, are often in a good position to facilitate this. But if they lose themselves by getting too immersed in running things from the centre, they no longer have the detachment or the sense of purpose to serve the community in this way.

Community development, in a church congregation as anywhere else, needs people who in this sense play a 'marginal' role, because the unofficial life of an institution, its informal networks, tensions, connections with the world outside, rivalries, hopes and sense of belonging, have the power to help or obstruct its avowed purposes, and also to generate the real energy for change.

'As watchmen wait for the morning so do our hearts wait for thee, O God.' It is those who exist on the periphery of a community, women like Mary and Anna as well as men like Elijah, who are traditionally its seers, rather than those who hold power at the centre. The ability to be a pastor is also closely associated with the ability to 'keep watch'. In the past this has usually been interpreted in terms of the clergy's function as guardians of communal morality in preaching, teaching and the exhortation of individuals. More recently, this aspect of leadership has been lost sight of altogether for fear of its authoritarian connotations. Furthermore, the modern pressure always to be busy and 'pastorally active' has obscured any image which carries with it the passive connotations of waiting for something to happen or watching while others work.

'Watching' also conflicts with the picture of pastoral action as always a matter of practical caring. Dreamers do not make good professional carers. Or do they? In recent years there has been more emphasis on the need for clergy to be good managers, as the decline in their numbers and the problems of maintaining church plant and encouraging greater commitment from congregations, have become more acute. They are encouraged to attend courses to gain management skills, to make parish audits and undergo periodic personal assessments in the name of greater accountability. This emphasis is understandable in a harsh climate in which inherited resources of wealth, goodwill and reputation have counted for less and less. But at the same time, it can lead to a rather obsessive concern for planning and for correct structures and there is a danger of beginning to value people only as potential recruits in the management programme rather than as free agents with a wealth of experience outside the immediate environs of church and church life.

The situation is made more complicated by the fact that it is less and less easy to define what is typical about different churches and pastoral situations, so that to import schemes and strategies from elsewhere is in itself a questionable activity. Hence the need for vision and a quality of discernment which draws its inspiration from close observation of the actual circumstances in which we are called to ministry, and the potential that is already there. The act of discernment is a communal one. Often it is a case of the minister attending to voices that were already present, especially those which cause discomfort and unease. The ordained minister, however, often plays a crucial role in determining what is brought into the light for scrutiny, and what is kept hidden.

In an article in the *Tablet* (4 May 1991) a Benedictine monk drew attention to the new thinking about business management emerging from the United States, and its relevance to the Church. The key phrases were 'participative management' and 'human resource management', and the good leader who could unlock latent potential in others was defined as someone with a strong sense of *vision* and the ability to communicate it. The managers themselves, rather than the work-force or the unions, were most often cited as the chief obstacle to progress in this direction, because of their tendency to become too busy and not to allow any time for reflection on the chief issues and the long-term view.

The professionalism of the ordained minister consists in a trained eye, rather than any claim to special knowledge and expertise. The experience of moving from one job to another often feels like relearning things from the start. But this experience, of constant re-vision and reflection, is the most valuable asset ordained outsiders can bring to the situation. In this sense also one may call them 'stewards' because they can bring out of their store of experience and reflection, ideas and insights, old and new, which may be useful to those among whom they work. They are also stewards in the sense that they have a special responsibility to keep the community in contact with the source of vision in worship.

Perhaps what we mean by pastoral leadership can be summed up in the old word 'oversight'. In the past this has been interpreted in an authoritarian way as denoting the person who checks up on others and makes sure that they are doing what they should. But, restoring it to the context of what it means to be a watcher and a shepherd, moving from place to place, perhaps we should note instead that the word implies someone who stays in a position where he or she can have an overall view of what is going on; which means staying on the edge, not being at the centre. This is necessary for the sort of insight to happen which facilitates change and growth.

8

MEETING ON THE ROAD:
PASTORAL CARE OF THE INDIVIDUAL

THE PASTORAL MINISTRY of the Church differs from other forms of professional advice and assistance in that it depends on a sharing of belief in the grace of God and a call to engage in struggle rather than self-edification or personal growth. It presupposes that grace is mediated at every level of life, not just the personal, but the social and communal as well; and that all forms of ministry, lay and ordained, point to this grace or uncover it in different ways by means of proclamation, challenge, forgiveness, strengthening and healing.

Since this belief is so central, it is interesting to ask oneself what episodes in the Gospels most clearly reveal for oneself *as a believer* the pastoral nature of Jesus' own ministry. Our answers may reveal what assumptions we work from in our own ministry.

When I was a university chaplain the story of the disciples on the road to Emmaus was the text which came to mean the most to me, because it seemed to characterize so well the situation I was in as a pastor to students. The story begins casually enough:

> That very day two of them were going to a village named Emmaus, about seven miles from Jerusalem, and talked with each other about all these things that had happened. While they were talking and discussing together, Jesus himself drew near and went with them. (Luke 24: 13–15 RSV)

As far as the disciples are concerned, their meeting with

Jesus is a chance encounter. As they are walking an apparent stranger meets them and starts tagging along. This detail alone typified the hit-and-miss nature of much of my pastoral ministry among students. My office was on one of the main corridors in the college. When I was in it I was aware of the constant flow of humanity outside. Like the students, I spent much of my time wandering from one part of the building to another. When I did so, I would always try to make time so that if someone stopped me, or even looked as if they might, I would have time to spend with them. You could call this form of ministry loitering with intent. In the same way as a burglar watches a house for a long time before he finds the right moment to enter it, I would make myself wait, often for a long time, until someone would allow a real conversation to take place. Often that conversation would not have taken place at all if there had not been a long sequence beforehand, progressing from glances, to smiles, to open acknowledgement and short conversations in the corridor. The moment of sudden ease or intimacy, when it came at all, was entirely unpredictable. Many of my most important pastoral exchanges came about in this odd and inconsequential way. No amount of advertising on student noticeboards, or in official literature, would have acted as a substitute for it.

I suppose my suspicion of professional modes of behaviour stem a lot from this experience of ministry. For example, most professional modes of behaviour involve meetings by appointment. The more appointments you have in your diary, the more you feel in demand as a professional. I was careful, at first unconsciously and then very self-consciously, *not* to have a diary with so many appointments that there was not the chance, if someone knocked on my door, that we could have time together there and then. It seemed important in an institution in which students and academics alike spent their time meeting appointments and deadlines, that the way I arranged my day pointed to different priorities. This form of ministry could be extremely frustrating. There were days when one felt one had achieved very little. And yet I would describe it as an active rather than a passive ministry. It required a special sort of attention to be able to take advantage of the pastoral opportunities when they arrived. Without the

awkward glances, the stilted conversations, the mutual embarrassment, the need for patience with the misapprehensions
people had about my role and the wish they had occasionally
to ridicule my supposed authority, these moments of ministry
would not have arrived at all.

Again this is something which connects with the story in
Luke 24. Jesus appears as a stranger and allows himself not
to be recognized at the outset, so that the recognition when
it comes is all the more powerful. What the story said to me
as a chaplain, was that I had to have the courage to remain
faithful to what in professional terms was an undervalued
form of ministry. In that way I might sometimes intervene in
another person's life in a way which revealed the presence of
Christ and brought about real change. In an increasingly
mobile society, when so many of our relationships with people
are fractured and temporary, and as pastors we come in, as
it were, half-way through a story, it is crucially important to
make sure that space is made for this sort of ministry, lay and
ordained.

Let us look more closely at the metaphors for ministry
contained in the story from Luke 24, and how they are
reflected in various forms of professional and non professional
care.

THE HELP OF STRANGERS

Being on the road immediately suggests the metaphor of pilgrimage, but the first thing to note is that while the disciples
are talking on the road, they are also at a point of crisis in
their own lives. The thing that had given meaning to their
lives has been taken away and they do not know what to do.
When Jesus meets them and asks them what they have been
talking about, Cleopas says 'Are you the only visitor to Jerusalem who does not know the things that have happened there
in these days?' and they express to the stranger their despair
at the loss of a messiah whom they *had* hoped was the one to
redeem Israel (vv. 17–21). This is a crisis of personal meaning
and future hope for the disciples. They are in despair because
now that their messiah has been proved false, in their eyes,

by the fact of his death they no longer have a goal in life provided by discipleship, and a way of patterning their hope for the future.

This relates directly to many pastoral situations. Very often we come into contact with people at a moment of crisis, or in its immediate aftermath. Very often this crisis involves more than one person in a sudden loss of purpose and meaning, and they find they cannot help each other without the involvement of someone else from apparently outside the situation. Usually the people involved have already made a reading of their situation which puts them into some sort of cul-de-sac. Often this is connected with an experience of loss. It may be a bereavement, but it could equally be the loss of a loved object such as a romantic attachment, a cherished belief about themselves or another, a job, or plans for retirement. The shattering of hopes for the future is as important, if not more so, than the pain of separation in the present.

The crucial part which this loss of meaning plays in the disciples' dilemma reminds us of the psychiatrist, Victor Frankl's emphasis on 'the will to meaning' being as important to human flourishing as the will for pleasure or power. Human existence, he wrote, 'is always directed to something or someone other than itself – be it a meaning to fulfil or another human being to encounter lovingly.[1] The meaning of the resurrection relates directly to this need, as the disciples' complaint to the stranger in this story makes plain. We may contrast the sense of loss and disorientation expressed in their first words to the stranger with their renewed vigour, purpose and sense of release at the end of the story when they recognize him for who he is. The same sense of loss fills Mary's cry to the supposed gardener outside the tomb, again in answer to the stranger's question: 'They have taken away my Lord, and I do not know where they have laid him' (John 20:13). In both cases the resurrection means to the bereaved, the restoration of their personal sense of purpose, meaning and future hope as well as the restoration of the one they loved. But in order to discover this they have first of all to accept the great change that has taken place. There is no going back to the situation before the cross and the tomb.

Viktor Frankl developed his thought as a result of the

almost mortal blow to his own sense of personal meaning and
that of other survivors of the entombment of European Jewry
in the Nazi concentration camps. He was himself an inmate
of Auschwitz and Dachau. It is not surprising therefore that
his thought relates so strongly to this story of the disciples on
the road to Emmaus. They too are survivors, but at an almost
unbearable cost. Many of the pastoral situations we become
involved in have this character. Other people may deal more
directly with the emergency which provoked the threat to
personal meaning. It may even be something that happened
a long time in the past. But we still deal with the aftermath
for the walking wounded.

Jesus' manner of approach to the disciples is very significant. He begins, not by announcing who he is, but by asking
them about themselves. In situations of personal crisis and
loss, what people need to do most of all is to tell their story.
Often they cannot tell it to people within their circle because
they feel the burden is too great, and so a friendly outsider
provides them with a new opportunity. They may have got
their situation totally wrong, and we, as the outsider with
greater knowledge, objectivity or faith, may see that they
have. But before we can contradict them or introduce another
interpretation we must first of all hear their own account.

So Jesus begins with a question. In the process of opening
the situation and their feelings about it to one they suppose
is a stranger and ignorant, the disciples begin to open themselves to change. Whereas their discussions so far have only
trapped them into going around in circles, the intervention of
this third party opens them to the possibility of seeing things
differently. The ministry provided by Jesus to the disciples is
challenging – it starts with a question – but at the same time
it is humble; it does not force recognition from the disciples
and preserves their freedom to react as they wish. To put this
in counselling terms, Jesus keeps his greater knowledge of the
situation in reserve. He allows the disciples to define the
situation for themselves first, and then begins to work on
changing it, still using the knowledge he shares in common
with them through the Scriptures. A key issue here is that of
personal freedom. Jesus could overrule the disciples. He
chooses not to, in the interests of provoking a change that,

when it comes, is all the more profound because it is unforced. This issue of respect for personal freedom is, as we have already noted elsewhere, one of the most critical for both pastoral care and evangelism.

Jesus helps the two disciples by getting them to tell their story first, and then reflecting it back to them, but in an altered context. In retelling the story he puts it into contact with the source of its meaning in Scripture:

> O foolish men, and slow of heart to believe all that the prophets have spoken! Was it not necessary that the Christ should suffer these things and enter into his glory? And beginning with Moses and all the prophets, he interpreted to them in all the scriptures the things concerning himself. (vv. 25–27)

I relate this in my own mind to how in some forms of therapy the counsellor enables the client to find direction by revealing a new meaning to the events that have already overtaken the person in the past.

There is a second aspect of the story I want to look at more closely. It is by keeping his personal identity a secret that Jesus helps the disciples. It is as a stranger and an outsider that he makes himself most available to them. While he is in this role he mirrors and reflects back to the disciples their own story and concerns, and reminds them of resources they already have at their disposal to help them (i.e., the scriptures and the interpretation that had been given to them in the life and teaching of Jesus when he was with them). In this hidden and unannounced way, Christ *incognito* acts representatively, in the sense that he represents and reflects back to the disciples a story which is already their own, if they could but see it. As soon as he is recognized for who he is, in the breaking of bread, he vanishes because his disciples no longer need his physical presence to assure them of the change that had indeed taken place.

It was my experience in chaplaincy especially, that in some pastoral encounters one was able to represent Christ in a way that paralleled this encounter between strangers on the road to Emmaus. For some sort of healing transaction to take place, it was not necessary that I should be previously known to the person seeking help, or that I should gain a very clear picture of what was at the root of their problem. Nor was it important that the person who came for help identified themselves as a believer or not. What was important on these occasions was that I should make myself available to listen, make evident by the sort of attention I gave to individuals that I stood alongside them, and should question them about their feelings and what they saw as possible ways forward. It astonished me how sometimes in one session of real listening, whether this had happened formally by appointment or through a chance encounter on a corridor, one could make a real difference to the way someone dealt with their situation. Reflecting on this, I explained it partly by the fact that students are in a transitional state between school and career, adolescence and maturity, or, if they are already adults, between one focus in life and another. This provided a context, which in my own mind I associated strongly with the theme of pilgrimage, where change could come quickly and be recognized for what it was. But I also realized that the very lack of a strong professional image on my part, my lack of a strong and incontestable role in the institution, made me available to take on whatever role might be necessary for a person to begin a dialogue. What particular knowledge, skill and insight I brought to a pastoral situation was not as important as what I reflected for the person in need.

If I had asked individuals why they had chosen to come to me, in many cases I am sure they would not have been able to give a clear answer. Belief of an open and committed kind on the part of the person who wanted to talk was not essential. Nor was the fact that I was clearly identified as an institutional representative of the Church by reason of my ordination. My lay colleagues in chaplaincy would have been able to point to similar experiences. On the other hand, a form of half-belief, a wish to believe, or a memory of belief was often important in serving to identify me as someone who might be trusted at times when a person had lost their capacity to put their trust in God directly. In this way one could become a channel between the individual and the presence of God hidden in their situation, however hopeless it might seem.

Personally, it did not seem to me to be important that the person helped or listened to should, as part of the encounter, be brought to the point where they could openly acknowledge they had been helped by God. Only that there should be the possibility left of some such recognition in the future. To me this indicates a more profound trust in the providence of God and the work of the Spirit than an attitude which insists on an open acknowledgement as the be-all and end-all of every pastoral encounter.

PASTORS AND COUNSELLORS

The pastor and the psychotherapist have in common that in the 'client's' eyes they are often seen as people without a clear individual identity of their own. They are intermediaries, putting the individual in contact with powerful sources of support and direction, through their association with hidden religious or psychological knowledge. They are mirrors which reflect back to a person their own situation, enabling them to gain a firmer grasp of their predicament and their hidden potential for change and growth. In this way both the pastor and the psychotherapist assist a person in their own healing by making them aware of the hidden potential for change already present in their situation. The pastor and the psychotherapist both deliberately limit the effect of their professional persona in order to allow the 'client' to make projections and assumptions about their role which may be important in the course of healing. There are differences, which we will come to in a moment, but in both cases, their helping role is gradually built up in the course of negotiation with the client, in the course of which they may have to adopt provisionally many different personae at the client's suggestion. In this way one could say that both roles are *answerable* to the client, in ways which other professions which concentrate on the functions they perform are not. Their ability to be answerable in this way depends on the very vagueness and softness of outline of the professional image.

In psychotherapeutic counselling this playing with roles is quite self-consciously made part of the process of healing. The whole way the sessions are arranged is deliberately created to enhance the process. The counsellor deliberately limits the amount the client talks, especially at the beginning of a relationship. Clues to the counsellor's personal character and circumstances are kept to a minimum. The client is met at prearranged times in a room which is usually warm and pleasant, but fairly anonymous. In the course of therapy, the counsellor proceeds by asking, 'What is this person projecting on to me and what connection may this have with the image they carry within themselves of past or present relationships?' and 'What am I feeling in this situation, and is this something I am being made to feel by the client, or something that comes because they have made contact with my own history and I have identified with one of the characters in their story?' This process of transference and counter-transference actually forms the content of therapy. The psychotherapeutic relationship provides a safe context for the playing out of roles and emotions that are experienced by the client as destructive and frightening outside.

A similar process often occurs in pastoral relationships, though it is not drawn attention to in the same way. For example, somebody may begin to talk by saying, 'I know I'm not a good Christian, but I've always believed in something.' Already in that remark the person is trying to establish a bond with the pastor, and projecting something on to the pastor with which he or she may personally feel uncomfortable and wish to correct – in this case, the image of the 'good Christian'. It is important that the pastor accepts the projection for the time being, and uses it as a means of exploring what image the individual making the remark has of goodness, and how they feel they have become separated from it. We can destroy the potential for a relationship by stepping in too quickly with reassurance or advice. Often the assumptions made by a person in distress about what we can do are wildly unrealistic. Sometimes we are made the recipients of the anger they wish to direct against God, or against all the people who have hurt them in the past. It is also sometimes true that the more hurt individuals have received from others, the more manipulative they become themselves.

All this is difficult for the pastor or the psychotherapist

to sustain. No wonder attention is sometimes drawn to the psychological complexity of wanting to be in this sort of helping role in the first place. The doctor and the lawyer may regard the personal feelings of the patient or the client, and their own feelings about them, as irrelevant to the task in hand. The pastor and the psychotherapist are not allowed this distance between their personal feelings and the claims their role makes on them. In a sense their own feelings are their instrument of research, the tools of their trade. This is what constitutes their availability, rather than any fantasy about always being on hand. This is the pattern through which the authority and experience they have gained through training and reflection is laid open as a form of service; and it is what makes the service a costly one.

This similarity of roles implies a similarity in basic attitudes. It is no surprise that many Christians are involved in psychotherapy, and that insights in this field have become more generally part of the pastoral and teaching ministry of the Church. The importance placed by psychotherapy on the sense of self and personal fulfilment is similar to the basic Christian belief in the importance of every individual as someone with an eternal destiny, for whom Christ died. The assumption that we can, by an act of imaginative sympathy, put ourselves in another's place, or that at bottom we share a basic humanity as ensouled creatures, is common to both approaches. Both are in one sense anti-materialist. To say that it is possible by empathy to reach an understanding of another's position, in spite of the great differences in how individual lives are formed by family, social and cultural circumstances, is to go beyond what would be regarded as feasible by many rationalists and materialists. Many would argue, however, that such an attitude, which is basically religious, is at the heart of *all* helping professions – those of teaching, medicine and social case-work, as well as pastoring and counselling.

The poet Keats, who in his short life was also training to be a doctor as well as writing poetry, saw this act of empathetic understanding as 'negative capability'. Working at a time when the scope for making certain diagnoses in physical medicine was much more limited than it is today, he wrote that what was needed most of all, by the medical student as well as the poet, was 'sensation [what we would call feeling] and watchfulness'. In Keats' day, when it had become possible to discern certain medical regularities but at the same time medical knowledge was not sufficiently systematized, the doctor had to proceed by *feeling his way*. To reach a true diagnosis he needed to have the imagination to put himself in the position of the patient and to remain in the state 'of being in uncertainties, Mysteries, doubts, without any irritable reaching after facts and reason'. This is what Keats defined as negative capability.[2]

Psychological knowledge has not yet reached the state of certainty of physical medicine, and religious knowledge is by its nature not capable of the sort of verification demanded by science, so it is not surprising that those seeking to act on the basis of psychological insight or religious faith should share a lot in common. Jung defined a quality very similar to negative capability when he wrote of a sort of discernment which should not be confused with purely intellectual, abstract thinking. He wrote:

> It is a human quality – a kind of deep respect for the facts, for the man who suffers from them, and *for the riddle of such a man's life* [my emphasis]. The truly religious person has this attitude. He knows that God has brought all sorts of strange and inconceivable things to pass and seeks in the most curious ways to enter a man's heart. He therefore senses in everything the unseen presence of the divine will. That is what I mean by 'unprejudiced objectivity'.[3]

This state of willed uncertainty is embodied in the mode of procedure which reflects back to the client various projections and representations rather than requiring acquiescence to a superior level of certain knowledge which the practitioner possesses as a professional.

Nobody can deny or undervalue the huge difference that has been made to human happiness by the adherence of modern medicine to rational, scientific procedures, but doctors themselves are coming to realize that the professional culture that has developed alongside this advance in knowledge has led to a neglect of the patients' role in their own healing and the doctor's ability to encourage this. Often this aspect of healing is left to others in the hospital, like the nurses and assistants, or the patient's own friends and family. The pastoral care of individuals, and counselling, both point in different ways to the process of healing as a 'making whole', which includes the patient's reaction to his or her own predicament and restoration to community with others as well as the provision of a solution for a physical problem. The position of the pastor or psychotherapist in this process is one of mediation.

SOME DIFFERENCES

Both the pastor and the psychotherapist may identify with Jesus' role as the stranger towards the two disciples on the road to Emmaus, uncovering common sources of knowledge and personal meaning, acting as a mirror for their deepest hopes and fears. But there are differences as well as similarities. One detail which intrigues me about the story is that it is only after Jesus has left them that the disciples are able to say who he was and how they had been helped. Up to the moment of recognition the relationship is apparently casual and accidental. Another detail, even more significant, is that the moment of recognition comes in a communal act of worship. Reflecting back from that moment on the rest of the story, we can see that what Jesus has been doing throughout is putting the disciples back into contact with communal sources of knowledge and insight. What has this to say about the differences between pastoring and counselling?

Jung himself realized that it was the space left by the decline of communal forms of religious faith that provided the social circumstances for the growth of psychoanalysis. In common with sociologists like Weber he believed that Protestantism, with the split it had introduced to the human psyche between faith and reason and its emphasis on the loneliness of the individual soul before God, had been largely responsible for this. So in seeking analogies for his own work as a psycho-

analyst he went behind the Protestant picture of the clergyman
as preacher and moralist emphasizing religious duties and service, to the older picture of the priest as confessor, healer and
mediator of unseen realities. At the same time he saw that it
was not possible in the new circumstances to reproduce what
had been done before. The social circumstances and education
of the patients he dealt with made it impossible to appeal to
communal faith and practice. For this reason he attempted
in a much more deliberate and self-conscious way to provide
access to the inner sources of healing in the individual and
collective unconscious – the same sources in his view represented in communal form in religious myths and ritual. The
individual and the analyst together could construct a path to
the development of a personal myth leading to integration. In
contrast to the role of the priest in the confessional, who was
able to put an individual in contact with the source of healing
simply by means of a communal sacrament, the healing in
the psychotherapeutic relationship occurred as the result of a
personal relationship with the analyst.

One could argue that Jungian analysis was itself a response
to Protestant individualism. It is no accident that psychotherapeutic modes of counselling flourish most among those
sections of society where the habits of individual self-help are
most ingrained and the means to supply it may be readily
found without the obstacles presented by poor social circumstances and education. Jung was conducting a battle on two
fronts: on the one side against the theories of Freud and Adler,
which he saw as being too much bound by the premises of
nineteenth-century science, therefore not giving enough room
for spiritual aspirations and the need for meaning; and on the
other against the oppressive force of religiously sanctioned
(Protestant) moralism. It is clear that he had in view the
educated who had left organized religion and were most open
to the new scientific theories. For them there could be no way
back to the old ways provided by religious faith and ritual.
They had, therefore, to find out for themselves the way to
personal fulfilment through an individual search.

So, paradoxically, Jung advised the use of analytical psychology as the means of re-establishing the pastoral bond
between the (Protestant) minister and his flock. But at the

same time he pointed to the power that communal rituals and symbolism had had as a means of providing healing.

> Any sacral action, in whatever form, works like a vessel for receiving the contents of the unconscious. Puritan simplification has deprived Protestantism of just this means of acting on the unconscious . . . There can be no doubt that the psychoanalytical unveiling of the unconscious has a great effect. Equally, there can be no doubt of the tremendous effect of Catholic confession, especially when it is not just a passive hearing, but an active intervention.[4]

What Jung looked forward to has already occurred. Analytic psychology has been used in many churches as the means of re-establishing the bonds of pastoral care. Whether it is in the area of spiritual guidance and self-discovery, bereavement counselling, marriage guidance or other examples of personal crisis, the model provided by the relationship contracted between an individual and psychotherapeutic counsellor tends to dominate. For many clergy in particular, this model is attractive as a way of getting round some of the difficulties and confusion that surround other aspects of their pastoral task. But, for the reasons which Jung himself draws attention to, we should be cautious of giving too exclusive attention to this form of care, thereby neglecting other aspects of the pastoral task and other ways of doing it.

Not everyone wants this form of assistance. As Jung implies, if someone is sufficiently in contact with communal sources of healing in religious symbolism and ritual, healing may be mediated directly without the self-conscious process which counselling implies. In many situations the person identified as a person of faith – often someone ordained, but it could be a member of the congregation or a particular neighbour or relative – can by their very presence act as a channel for a healing interaction to take place. It does not always have to be verbalized, put into a formal context – whether that of the confessional or the counselling session – nor formally acknowledged. As Jung's own emphasis on the importance of ritual and symbol suggests, we should pay equal attention to unverbalized means of pastoral care and support. There is a whole area of human contact between the ritually formalized gestures of public occasions and the purely personal and intimate gestures of private life, in which we can give support by what we do as well as what we say. Often in a situation we will be given cues about how we are expected to behave nonverbally, what gestures we can use, what can be conveyed by silence and touch.

If we concentrate so much on structured conversations as the means of conveying pastoral care, we neglect other opportunities given to us when this is not possible. Clergy are often frustrated by less than ideal conditions in which they are asked to minister pastoral care – in the living room with the television on, in the street with children tugging at a person's arm, in a crowded hospital ward or at a family gathering. They forget that most people operate under these conditions for most of the time, and that it is under these conditions they give each other support.

As pastors we should be grateful for the insights provided by psychotherapy, but not bound by its mode of practice. For example, the idea of a formal session conducted in a special place at a prearranged time is alien to many people. It has all the wrong connotations of being interviewed or examined. They may clutch hold of your arm and pour out their heart to you in a pub, with enough noise around them to mask the transaction, but if you asked them to keep an appointment in your house or theirs, they might clam up immediately. The procedures of psychotherapy have been developed in a particular social milieu and do not necessarily translate well into other contexts. In an area where there is a very transitory population, where many people cannot predict what their life will be like in a few weeks, let alone a few years, and whose family commitments and patterns of work make it impossible to keep the same pattern of appointments over a period of time, the knowledge that they could drop into a church or a hall, finding it open and somebody there, without the need to make a telephone call or to be referred, might be a far more appropriate expression of pastoral care than having a team in the congregation designated as having counselling skills. The two approaches are not mutually exclusive, but as a matter of pastoral priority, it might be important to first make the church more open and accessible, before considering the training of individuals as counsellors. Finally, the practice of counselling presupposes a particular kind of articulacy. The ability to listen, to interpret what someone is saying and reflect it back to them taking into account their possible reaction, places a lot of emphasis on the verbal and intellectual skills of the counsellor and the client. If we take the counselling model as the yardstick in discerning who in a congregation might have special pastoral gifts, we may overlook other expressions of imaginative sympathy which are equally valid.

BACK TO COMMUNITY

The whole counselling tradition up until now has been highly individualistic, both in origin and development. It assumes contact between two individuals only, the counsellor and the client, and the 'drama' of therapy, the catharsis or change it brings about in an individual, is a purely internal one. In many ways it fits in with the whole tone of modern living, in which most individuals are limited to a very small set of significant relationships. But, as Jung himself recognized, the Church, at least in the Catholic understanding, is a sign and expression of a much wider sense of community, based not only on face-to-face relationships between individuals, but on contact with suprahuman and supranatural reality. Therefore, in the provision of pastoral care, we should also be as aware of the communal and more-than-individual ways in which this care is conveyed, particularly in worship. Robin Green has highlighted the ways in which public worship can directly promote or hinder pastoral care, in his book *Only Connect*.[5] Worship includes the more-than-verbal. The details of how people are seated, how they greet each other, what non-verbal expressions are encouraged, or discouraged, the silences, the balance of formality and informality, as well as what images of God and of human life are promoted in the preaching and liturgical texts, are all pastorally significant. If people feel that they are included in worship, that their particular situation

in life is being addressed, then they will gain the confidence
to become pastorally active. If, however, they feel excluded,
overlooked or rooted to the spot, they will not feel able to
express their gifts in pastoral ways either.

The pastor is both more *and* less free in relation to the
individual seeking help and advice than is the counsellor. This
is because of an underlying difference in how their individual
ministry is related to community. The pastor is *more* free,
in that a relationship with the individual has already been
established because of the presence of the community of faith.
For the same reason the focus for the pastoral relationship
does not have to be a problem, nor does the pastor need to
wait for the individual to initiate the contact. Something is
already assumed about their role, drawn from their actual
relationship to a community. The pastor does not have to
draw attention to his or her own relationship to the individual.
Often neither the pastor nor the individual is entirely aware
of what help is being given. What is taking place is between
the individual and God, or the community of faith, or a
particular human grouping – the family, neighbours, the local
church – *through* the pastor. And this often happens by virtue
of the actual relationship the pastor enjoys with the community. It is not entirely a matter of what the individual
projects on to the pastor in the course of their relationship;
which is one reason why these projections do not have to be
focused on explicitly as part of the process of giving help.
Unlike counselling relationships, in a pastoral relationship it
is unnecessary for the pastor to hide other relationships, either
with other individuals or the community. Indeed, it is part of
the pastor's mediating role that they should be included. This
is central to what we mean by the ministry of reconciliation.

On the other hand, and for the same reasons, the pastor is
not as free as the counsellor. The pastoral relationship is not
a contract between two individuals for specific purposes which
are primarily those of the client. The pastor is not free to
leave outside the relationship norms and ideals which belong
to the community. These form the 'tradition' which it is part
of the pastor's role and skill to bring into living contact with
the other person's need for individual freedom of conscience
and choice. Neither the pastor nor the individual can ignore

this background, though they may interpret it. In fact it is the area of mediation between communal tradition and individual cases which forms the content of pastoral theology. The authority of the individual pastor depends on his or her ability to make fruitful contact between the tradition and individual needs.

This is a different process from encouraging someone to arrive at an answer to their predicament by self-discovery, with the counsellor as non-directive companion. So, for example, in the case of a contemplated divorce, a counsellor's help might be based on arriving at an assessment of how mutually beneficial or destructive the individual relationship had been, what contract had been assumed by the couple in the marriage, and what potential for individual personal growth there was within it. But the pastor, whilst acknowledging these factors, would also have to give weight to communal and religious expectations of what marriage signifies, and the relationship between these two – the individual and the communal – might form the major content of the discussion.

Nor can pastoring aspire to be non-directive, or non-judgemental, in the sense that these terms are used in some forms of counselling. Every discipline has its own ideological roots. Pastoral guidance on the one hand, and non-directive forms of counselling on the other, have their roots in different theological strands which have been interwoven in Christian tradition from the beginning – the one biblical and redemptive, based on God's dealings with a people; the other mystical and Platonist in outlook, based on the divine presence within the individual soul. Psychotherapy is deeply influenced by the notion that true 'gnosis' or understanding is of itself of saving value. But, as Marx said, the aim is not to understand the world but to change it. The aim of the pastor is not necessarily to bring to light what is hidden, but to point to the gracious activity of God, both at the individual level and at the level of community, and to reflect that activity to individuals in a way that will bring comfort, challenge and reconciliation.

Jung developed his theories after a great deal of personal suffering and in conscious rebellion against the tyrannical moralism which his father, a Protestant minister, personified. The contribution which psychotherapy has to make to pastoral ministry is considerable and nowhere more so than in guarding against a return to the sort of moralism which crushes the spirit. Jung himself was very good at sniffing out moral tyranny masquerading as spiritual guidance. To quote him once more:

> In actual life it requires the greatest art to be simple, and so acceptance of oneself is the essence of the moral problem and the acid test of one's whole outlook on life. That I feed the beggar, that I forgive an insult, that I love my enemy in the name of Christ – all these are undoubtedly great virtues. What I do unto the least of my brethren, that I do unto Christ. But what if I should discover that the least amongst them all, the poorest of all beggars, the most impudent of all offenders, yea the very fiend himself – that these are within me, and that I stand in need of the alms of my own kindness, that I myself am the enemy who must be loved – what then? Then, as a rule, the whole truth of Christianity is reversed: there is then no more talk of love and long-suffering; we say to the brother within us 'Raca', and condemn and rage against ourselves.[6]

It worries me that many forms of individual pastoral care encourage this self-hatred. Having observed the sort of activity that went on among students under various terms, as 'discipling', 'shepherding', 'pastoring', and even 'Christian counselling', I have been made aware of the existence of very real dangers of offence against the sanctity of the individual conscience. How very different is this sort of patrolling of the individual for signs of deviation in the interests of group conformity from the walk Jesus took himself with his disciples on the road to Emmaus.

PAINFUL ENCOUNTERS:
PASTORAL CARE OF THE UNCHURCHED

WE HAVE COME BACK in this final chapter to the situation which began the book – the black limousine at the cemetery gates. How do we, as pastors, perform our role for unchurched people in a situation like this, in which many factors are beyond our control? How should we use the occasions like baptism, marriage, and funerals when the world of folk religion comes into contact with the world of organized religion? As evangelistic opportunities? As claims upon our professional services which cannot be ignored, but which are at some remove from the real focus for ministry? As a chance to revive in the community a sense of the Church which has all but disappeared? Actually, each of these questions already implies a judgement on folk religion: that folk religion is pagan and therefore not to be countenanced; that it is merely the after-glow of religious sentiment in a totally secularized culture; or that it is a real but implicit expression of a traditional faith which has always had a place for the Church and its ministry.

There is probably truth in all these statements. But they also reflect the pastor's anxiety about the role of the minister in circumstances which take him or her beyond the immediate congregation. So if they are imposed by a minister as a judgement on a particular pastoral situation, rather than something arising out of real reflection on that situation, they can all give rise to misunderstanding and resentment. For example, the minister who has put a family through a rigorous course of classes and attendance at church before she will baptize their child cannot understand why, when the baptism has taken place, they do not come to church again. Or the bereaved come back from a funeral feeling that the minister did not really care and the service was impersonal. Or a priest feels hurt and let down when the couple who welcomed him as the minister for their marriage treat him almost as a stranger when he calls on them again ,a few months afterwards.

In this chapter I want to look more closely at the presence of folk religion as a sometimes helpful, but at the same time complicating, factor in pastoral contact through the occasional offices of birth, marriage and death with those we term 'the unchurched'. But it should be made clear from the outset that a straightforward identification cannot be made between folk religion and the religion of the unchurched. The reasons why some individuals find a place in different churches and others do not, are very complicated and as much to do with social differences as differences in belief. One meets total non-churchgoers who nevertheless pray daily and are otherwise thoroughly orthodox. On the other hand, one is constantly surprised when accident reveals the variety of personal belief, superstition, agnosticism or even atheism present beneath the surface in the most ordinary church congregation.

The term 'folk religion' is potentially misleading because it implies something with which we are already familiar, something traditional and accessible (folk), and something relatively organized (religion). These are not fair assumptions about the varieties of belief and unbelief among the unchurched. The word 'folk', moreover, has patronizing connotations, putting some unchurched people's religion under scrutiny whilst ignoring others altogether. All of us 'suffer', if that is the right term, from various sorts of folk belief. Viewed in a detached way, the assumption made by some schools and parents that confirmation is a necessary adjunct to a good education, an accomplishment rather like learning to play an instrument, is as extraordinary as the idea that baptism protects a child from physical danger. But the latter opinion is much more likely to get categorized as an incorrect or 'folk' variation of belief than the former. How you define 'folk religion', therefore, depends very largely on your perspective. 'Pluralist structures of peoples' beliefs' would be a more accurate if more cumbersome term for the modern situation. In this chapter I will continue to use the shorter and better

known term, but many of the assumptions behind it need
challenging and explaining.

DRAWING THE LINE

The debate about folk religion is largely a debate about where
we draw the line between 'real' religion and the world of
unbelief or superstition.

Some people, whether Christian apologists or academic
sociologists, think that the real boundary is between what
happens inside and outside the church. What matters is the
number of people inside churches, and this is the only basis
on which one can measure the rise or decline of religious faith.

Others, who again include both Christian apologists and
secular critics of religion, see religion as a more constant
dimension of human experience which may or may not have
visible institutional expression and support. Religion is a universal sentiment, using this word in its strongest possible
sense, capable of a variety of expressions, some of them apparently secular or private, some of them organized, overtly
religious and public. In this view, where the boundaries are
drawn between what goes on inside and what goes on outside
the ecclesiastical umbrella is itself a major focus of concern.
The ecclesiastical umbrella only more or less corresponds to
what the sociologist Peter Berger called 'the Sacred Canopy',[1]
a term which embraces the totality of human awareness of
the transcendent, especially in the experiences of birth, chance
and decay, and death. To this way of understanding, folk
religion is as important as organized or denominational
religion, and the proximity or distance of its expression from
the church is one of the most fascinating questions of all.

The first view, whether it is mounted by apologists for
the Church or by its secular critics, portrays the boundaries
between real or organized religion and unreal, folk or secularized versions of it as either static, or always going in one
direction; the latter view recognizes that the boundaries are
always shifting between the two. What lies outside the boundaries of organized religion may be described, as by a colleague
of Berger's, Thomas Luckmann, as 'invisible religion';[2] but

this does not make it any the less real. The question must always be put, *invisible to whom?* We must recognize that the very term 'folk religion' is a coinage used by apologists for the Church and by academic sociologists for whatever touches on the *main* focus of their concern, whether this is the mission of the Church or the theory of secularization. It is only a partial definition for whatever swims into their ken, and not by any means an exhaustive definition of the religion of non-churchgoers.

In Luckmann's view, 'invisible religion' was not a negative term used to describe whatever falls outside the scope of organized religion as superstition, proverbial wisdom, philosophy or private belief, but a positive term pointing to humanity's reflexive capacity to transcend its biological state. This helps to account for the persistence of religion in secularized environments. It is an irreducible 'given' in social life, and productive of ever new forms of religious belief and behaviour. A similar conclusion was reached by David Hay on the basis of interviews with people who had answered the question: 'Have you ever felt as though you were very close to a powerful spiritual force that seemed to lift you out of yourself?'[3] The researchers found that such experience was very widespread, that it was nearly as common among the unchurched as among the churched, and even included a proportion who would still describe themselves as atheist. The experiences themselves were very varied, though many referred to situations of stress such as sickness, bereavement and extreme danger, and they happened more commonly when people were on their own. David Hay's conclusion was that something akin to Otto's 'sense of the holy' is part of our biological heritage. By its very nature it has the capacity to take us out of ourselves and to make us aware of the deeper dimensions to living. It is, furthermore, intimately connected with individual and social well-being.

The relationship between this level of experience and organized religion is a very complex one. Organized religion is in itself a response, an interpretative framework giving shape, power and meaning to the experience and helping to communicate it. At the same time, the uncontrolled nature of the experience is always a potential threat to religious conformity.

So religious authorities are left with a dilemma. They must keep in contact with this level of experience because otherwise the source of their own living worship and tradition will dry up. At the same time, especially in the context created by modern pluralism, if they open the door to it too wide, they lose their hold on the truth of their tradition. If they close the door on it, however, their life as a religious institution may become increasingly irrelevant and oppressive.

In a sense it comes down to a question of hospitality. People who have been given religious experiences are like people who have been issued with invitations to a feast, and religious institutions are like the hosts. Neither can act in total disregard of the other. If a church is not willing in any sense to entertain the beliefs and experiences of the unchurched, if it makes no room for them in its life, its ability to transcend the limits of its own life as an institution is diminished and eventually it ceases to make any space at all for a real sense of the holy. Seen like this, the pastoral care of the unchurched is a ministry of hospitality to the variety of their experience. At the same time hospitality is not possible without conventions governing the behaviour of guests and hosts alike. There are 'laws' of hospitality.

Individual religious experience finds expression in a variety of folk practices besides organized religion. The relationship with the latter has always been a problematic one. Knowing how to balance the demand for pastoral sensitivity with concern for theological integrity, has been a major task for Christian leadership since Christianity stopped being a Jewish sect and moved out into the wider Roman world. There has never been a golden age when organized and folk religion reflected one another perfectly. Furthermore, revival in the Church has often been accompanied by the redrawing of the boundaries between institutional religion and folk belief. In his famous book *Religion and the Decline of Magic*,[4] Keith Thomas makes clear that folk religious practices did not disappear in England under the impact of the Protestant Reformation and Puritanism. They simply went underground where they often took more bizarre form than before, totally unaffected by the prevailing norms of official belief. What *had* changed was the relationship with official belief which became much more antagonistic and fearful, resulting in the peculiarly seven-teenth-century phenomenon of witch-hunts. A study of folk religion in Lincolnshire in the nineteenth century[5] reveals how persistent folk practices remained, and how loosely they were associated with the local church, before the exodus to the towns in the Industrial Revolution made the links even more tenuous. Interestingly enough, this study is based on evidence some of which is drawn from the writings of local clergymen who, under the impact of the Evangelical and Catholic revivals in the Church of England, became more concerned for the mission of the Church to ordinary people. Committed pastoral care led them to a discovery of their own ignorance of prevailing patterns of belief and practice. Wesleyanism and the various Methodist revivals at different times and in different parts of the country, profoundly affected popular belief and attitudes to Christianity. Revival, Sunday schools and teetotalism stimulated a further separation between the culture within church congregations and outside them. At the same time they profoundly influenced popular notions of what religion was. There is a wealth of history behind casual remarks like 'You don't smoke, do you, Vicar? It's against your religion.'

So the relationship between Christianity and folk religion is not a simple one. It takes very different shapes in different ages, countries, cultures and denominational hinterlands. There has never been a time in the history of Christianity when the faith has been entirely coterminous with a particular culture, but nor can it remain entirely foreign to any culture if it is to take root and develop. This is the dilemma that faces every pastor when stepping away from the immediate circle of the congregation and seriously engaging with the complex-ities of faith and unbelief among people outside.

Working in a multi-racial part of south London has made me painfully aware of these complexities. 'Folk religion' is useful only as a form of shorthand for clergy and sociologists to communicate with each other. To take it any more seriously as a term would be to give to the various expressions of belief outside the churches a spurious unity they do not in fact possess. The differences where I work are so glaringly obvious that as a pastor I am forced to take them into account, but my experience here has also led me to question my responses in previous pastoral contexts where the differences were not so close to the surface. For one group of people, what *I* call folk religion may be a highly organized complex of taken-for-granted assumptions, beliefs and rituals in which not just the family but their whole network of friends and relatives is involved. For me as a pastor, coming in from the outside, their world may seem, to begin with, almost impenetrable, particularly if the situation is complicated by ethnic difference; but once the language of signs and symbols and fragments of religious speech has become more familiar, it is easy enough to discover what role has been assigned to me. I may not choose to fulfil the role exactly as the family has decided, but at least it has given me a basis for negotiation. In this situation, my problem is basically one of ignorance. Once I have learnt to move around in the family's world with more confidence, things will get easier. So, for instance, if at a Caribbean funeral, I know the family is likely to expect that the coffin should remain open in church, that family members and friends make speeches during the service and that there will be singing at the graveside; or if, after a baptism, I know I will be expected to bless the table at the family's home, I will be saved from making elementary mistakes, and know I can help in the mediation of support and faith to the families concerned.

On the other hand, I can easily overestimate the presence of understood ways of belief and behaviour in families which are different from my own. I may discover, on another occasion, that there is nothing explicit in terms of belief or understood ways of behaviour, and a great deal of disagreement and embarrassment among family members. This situation is much more complicated because hardly any cues are given to me as to how I am expected to behave. Often I will be taken by surprise by the power of the feelings which my presence in the midst of the family evokes. Here my problem is not so much one of ignorance as of sensitivity. If I am not aware how far the feelings expressed towards me are bound up with individuals' projections on to God, the Church or religion, and so on to me as their representative, I can easily feel personally hurt or insulted by the degree of avoidance, guilt, fear and outright hostility in the way I am treated. On one level the family may be asking me to take control of the situation, while on another level individuals attack me for doing so. Thus, for example, a family will want me to show how seriously I take the matter of their child's baptism, but regale me at the same time with all sorts of negative arguments about God ('If God's so good, why does he let children/animals suffer?' is a common one), the Church (usually on the lines that not many people go to church nowadays and the people who do are hypocrites) and my own role (for example, 'Vicars used to be special in the old days. You used to be afraid of them. But now it's just a job for you, isn't it?'). Unless I am aware of the degree to which this double message is caused by the family's own insecurity about how they will be received, I will easily fall into the trap of countering their apparent rejection with anger and cynicism about their motives.

The projections are not always negative. Sometimes a pastor can be taken aback by their positiveness. It is equally dismaying to be treated as a god as a devil. Used to seeing themselves as professional carers or institutional representatives, ministers can be taken aback when suddenly given a charismatic authority they do not really want. And yet for people with little or no formal contact with the Church as an institution, it often comes naturally to do just that. I come across this occasionally when someone contacts me suddenly because they feel there is a bad atmosphere, or a ghost, in their house, or that they have been marked out for bad luck. It can be disconcerting to discover how much value is placed on one's prayers as someone associated with a sense of the holy. One is fearful of encouraging magical and instrumental notions of religion. And yet to refuse a response, or to immediately suggest there is something wrong with the person rather than their circumstances, can often create lasting hurt. As pastors, we become so used to the world of our own denomination, we forget that for many, perhaps the majority of people, religion is based on claims to experience, personal example and a sense of something holy. It takes an effort of imagination for us to realize the impact that a church building, a religious person or an act of worship can have on someone who is not acquainted with them. But if we look back, perhaps, at what has been important to us in the growth of our own faith, we will not find this sense of religion, as something attached to particular places and people, so unusual after all.

BACK TO THE CEMETERY

What has been said above may help to mitigate the distance separating organized religion from the religion of the unchurched. But several factors have combined to make us, as pastors today, particularly conscious of the distance between common assumptions and beliefs within congregations and the range of assumptions and beliefs we meet with outside.

First of all there is the general privatization of religion. It is not just organized religion which has been affected by this trend in our society. This came home to me forcibly a year ago when a lecture made me think about graveyards, and in particular the difference between the graveyard in the village where I was trained and the cemeteries I visit now. My theological college was unusual in that the principal of the college was also the vicar of the village church. Apart from the students, the service was largely attended by the local farmers, professionals and retired people. The real villagers, many of whom worked in the college, were largely absent except for a smattering of children who were serving or being prepared for confirmation. However, around the church was a very well-tended churchyard. Though the village was not well represented in the congregation, the churchyard was its own. Here the network of the village, largely invisible to the eyes of outsiders, was exposed. A careful scrutiny of the names on the graves would have revealed which family was related to whom by blood and marriage and how long they had been in the village, as well as some of their private tragedies. At the end of the service, as we filed out of the church, already a couple of villagers might be in the churchyard tending their family's graves, and this number would increase during the Sunday afternoon.

Where I work now, local people must travel at least four

to five miles to the nearest cemetery, and this has always been true from the time this area ceased to hold just a few big houses and became a proper suburb. Our church, originally built as a convenient place to hold Sunday services in 1793, has never had a churchyard. This visible link between the churched and the unchurched has been severed by a physical dislocation of the graveyard from the church – a disruption to the relationship between the church and local society which is already nearly two hundred years old! It took me a couple of years here, picking up on chance remarks made by people within and outside the congregation, before I realized that the cult of the dead was perhaps as vibrant here as it had been in the village. I have discovered that many families will cross London on a Saturday or Sunday to tend graves, or sit down in crematoria gardens to remember and often to talk to their dead. But this happens beyond sight of a church and without any attachment to denominational religion.

This is a dramatic visual symbol of the change that has occurred between the church and folk religion. In the village they were in some proximity to each other. The villagers tended their graves within the shadow of the church. In this part of London they are usually unrelated. It is not just that the link with the church has been broken, but that this is indicative of a general loss of community. Friends and neighbours, too, may remain entirely unaware of the outings someone makes to a municipal cemetery and what they do when they get there, whereas in the village tending graves was to some extent a public activity. The religion of the unchurched has not disappeared so much as been *relocated* to a private sphere which is not as accessible or visible to interested outsiders, including pastors. A lot of what is taken to be the disappearance of religion in our society today is due not to its removal by the onslaught of secular forces but to its relocation. Not secularization, therefore, so much as privatization of religion – a process which affects the sphere of organized religion inhabited by churchgoers as much as the religion of the unchurched – is the factor that has most affected the relationship between church, or churchgoing, and society.

Secondly, both organized and folk religion have been seriously affected by the collapse of public codes of behaviour and the disruption of stable communities, and their substitution by imagined notions of belief and community drawn from contact with close friends and the media. How, for example, does one assess the waves of emotion that sweep through the nation at times of crisis like the Falklands war or the Gulf war? Six million people watch *Songs of Praise*. But who knows what each of those six million individuals makes of what they see and hear?

For someone living within the world of organized religion, this relocation of religion away from visible local expression and into the living room and on to the TV screen comes as a tremendous shock, particularly for pastors in their care of the unchurched. Because so much now happens behind locked doors and is not publicly in association with a local church or community, we approach each contact, when taking a funeral for example, not knowing what to expect. At one level we may find among the unchurched deeply conservative beliefs about death, hell and punishment, the stock-in-trade of preachers fifty to a hundred years ago, but not so current even among theological conservatives today. At another level we may meet versions of scientific rationalism based on the nineteenth-century debate between science and religion. (How often, for instance, one is asked the question 'Do you believe in Evolution?' – what a very significant choice of words, especially in the context the word 'believe'.) In both these examples the religion of the unchurched has preserved fragments of traditional faith or old arguments which have been forgotten in current forms of organized religion – a fact of crucial importance to recognize when learning how to deal with people's beliefs and the projections they make on to the Church.

On yet another level, we meet deep currents of fatalism or superstition which have always remained relatively untouched by Christianity in whatever form. Folk religion can be extremely conservative. On the other hand it can equally be extremely innovative. Novel religious factors which organized Christianity is hardly as yet in contact with, have made deep inroads into people's beliefs outside the Church. Ask yourself how often someone has revealed to you a tentative belief in reincarnation, or how deeply we are all affected by psychotherapeutic notions and techniques for self-realization, and you will see how subtle are the transactions which are continuously taking place between the different systems of belief within our society and forces outside. Ironically, though some Christians bitterly attack the sorts of philosophy associated with the term 'New Age', their own faith is deeply influenced by the same notions of realizing their full potential and harnessing spiritual energies which form the focus of much of what they attack.

Both the relocation and the privatization of folk religion make great difficulties for the pastor. We cannot assume we know what is going on in individual situations. Whereas, previously, the proximity of folk religion to the local church meant that there might be a relationship of interdependence, because to some extent they were part of the same world and might legitimately sustain each other, the distance which now separates them has become a real problem. And it brings with it other pastoral problems as well as those born of ignorance, of which the most important is the problem of control.

The ill feeling which sometimes surrounds contact between clergy and the unchurched in those brief moments when they are brought into contact is often caused by the pastor's awareness of their own lack of control over how the religious contribution they are called upon to make is going to be interpreted and appropriated. Pastors often compensate for this by defining as clearly as possible the boundaries between what is of the faith and what is not. But no one is in absolute control of religious meanings in modern society, so that any bid for control by church representatives which ignores the other voices present in a particular situation is bound to fail. The Church of England has found this out, for example, in relation to the remarriage of divorced people. The Church is simply not in control of the social contexts in which marriages break up or survive. This presents it with a pastoral and theological dilemma. Either it must maintain a rigid policy which will prevent it from coming in contact with many people at a critical time in their lives. Or, because of the wide powers of discretion given to its ministers, individual clergy may effectively adopt a 'members only' policy, making the personal faith of the couple the prime consideration. Or the Church recognizes that it must find new ways of relating to a situation in which many stay out of wedlock altogether, and many have experiences of marriages which have failed.

Much of the present confusion, which causes so much pain in individual encounters, is caused by the refusal of the Church to act in the recognition that other voices and authorities are present as well as its own. The Church does not have to agree with these other voices, but it cannot behave as if people come through some sort of air lock or decompression chamber when they make an approach to the Church, which immediately separates them from the atmosphere of life as it is lived on the outside. At the local level, the pastor always has to recognize that he or she is often acting in competition with other voices and authorities, whether it is the local undertaker, what people read in the papers or other members of the family. Hence the little nod I make to the monument as I pass through the cemetery gates.

THE NEED FOR CONTROL

Much of the pain that surrounds pastoral contact with the unchurched seems to me to be caused by covert attempts by the churches to gain more control in an uncertain area of mission under the apparently neutral headings of liturgical change and better pastoral practice. Take, for example, the new forms of service for baptism and funerals in the Church of England. In these new services the lines are much more clearly drawn around what is considered to be the faith of the Church and what is not. This reflects the change in the position of the Church in society. Whereas the old versions assumed that the people who used the offices might share a common understanding of what the services meant, nowadays such an assumption is considered unrealistic. Christian teaching was contained in the old liturgies in the form of exhortations to remember what was known already. The new versions, on the other hand, are less exhortatory and more clearly didactic in tone. So for example, whereas the Book of Common Prayer service for the public baptism of infants immediately launches the worshipper without preamble into the scriptural imagery of sin and regeneration, and leaves the duties of godparents to the end, the liturgy for the baptism of children in the Alternative Service Book *begins* with the duties of parents and godparents, and makes it clear that the sponsors are to declare their *own* faith as well as stand surety for the child. The need of the individual child to be washed from sin is played down in comparison with the old service. On the other hand the whole theme of joining the 'family of the church' is played up, and crucially underlined in the prayer of welcome said by the whole congregation. This all implies a different, and on the whole negative, attitude to the religion of the unchurched. It has to be made clear to them from the start that what is happening is not so much a mystical or magical washing for the child's protection – a 'folk' form of belief that the old prayer book service might encourage rather than challenge – as joining a new family in which new duties and obligations will be expected of them and their sponsors.

Similarly, the new burial service begins with a prayer for the strengthening of faith, emphasizes the centrality of Christ in the process of salvation, and rejects the comforting and inviting words of the old collect for a more explicit call for repentance and discipleship. The old service is full of a sense of sorrow and regret for the brevity of life – something which immediately connects with the feelings and fears of the mourners. The new service, though apparently more gentle, gives much less room for these feelings.

I am suggesting that a hidden theme of much liturgical revision has been the distance the Church perceives between the faith it proclaims and what may be brought to its worship in the way of vague understanding and folk belief by the unchurched. The very obscurity of the language of the old services made them more amenable to whatever constructions the worshipper wished to put upon them. The intention behind the new words is much clearer, and for that reason more at the control of the minister than the worshipper. The unchurched or occasional worshipper is not even left the Lord's Prayer in a version they may half remember. It is interesting how, in merely going through the new baptism service with a family, one is already pushed towards adopting a more closed rather than open policy to baptism. The service begins with our agenda rather than that of the family, and that determines the tone throughout.

Argument between clergy and laity about liturgical changes forms one of the well-worn themes of church life today. It is easy for clergy, sure of their ground theologically, to become impatient with various groups of laity, some of them very well placed, but others, as in the case of most of the unchurched, very badly placed, to make their unease about the changes known. Behind many of the disagreements there is an ideological struggle concerning what the Church is, and it is the unwillingness of the clergy to recognize this which often leads to pastoral insensitivity. I say ideological rather than theological struggle, to highlight the element of covert manipulation in such areas as liturgical change, whether initiated at a local or national level, which works to exclude some notions of what the Church is in favour of others, to the extent that the latter are seen as being the *only* ones that are possible or legitimate. Usually these changes are defended as being more pure or more authentic, and the social and ideological reasons for needing images which assert strong boundaries between insiders and outsiders are ignored. Whilst I agree that these reasons may be compelling, I feel they should be openly asserted and argued about rather than hidden in liturgical revision.

There is a case for arguing that some forms of folk religion contain equally powerful notions about what the Church is. For instance, the connection between being a Christian and being a citizen which was assumed by virtually all parties when the Book of Common Prayer was written, is still very strong in some forms of folk religion. Hence the sense of outrage, that I or my baby is not considered good enough, evoked when clergy explain to the unchurched who come forward for baptism that personal Christian commitment is shown primarily by church attendance and not – though this is usually not stated openly – by one's intention to behave well as a citizen or a parent. This becomes particularly acute when there may be other reasons – class difference or illegitimacy, for example – which from the family's point of view affect the clergyman's attitude.

The unchurched may not be able to articulate to the clergyman's satisfaction what they think the Church is. That does not mean that there is no theological undergirding to their point of view. A professional pastor caught up in conflict over a child's baptism may characterize it as one of conflict between theological principle and pastoral concern. In this way he or she automatically denies from the outset that the views of the unchurched have any theological standing. In point of fact, the conservative nature of much folk religion means that in some cases it preserves elements of traditional teaching which the Church today finds it necessary to ignore or play down. On occasion the Church is no more consistent in its point of view than its critics. It denies the link between baptism and a person's status as a citizen, for example, and yet defends its share in public education which requires baptism as a condition of entry. The unchurched parent is often well aware that, in this regard at least, there is a practical link between baptism and citizenship. Furthermore, though many clergy adopt a strict policy towards baptism, few would adopt a similar policy regarding funerals. The reasons for not doing so are as much sociological as they are theological. In practice we operate in accordance with different notions of the Church depending on whether the context is birth, marriage or death. Outsiders may be at a loss to understand why distinctions applied in one context do not apply in the same way in others. Why, for instance, if I am allowed to be married in church, won't the same priest baptize my baby when the time comes?

The more we enquire into the relationship between the Church and folk religion, the more we begin to see the true usefulness of the term, 'the unchurched', but this time as a way of focusing on the activity of the institutional Church in drawing boundaries for its own purposes, rather than for making any immediate judgement on the state of belief among those thus defined as outside. Folk religion contains many different strands, some of them totally alien to any recognizable expression of Christianity, but others embodying elements of teaching and tradition rejected by the Church, perhaps only for a time. The boundaries are constantly shifting. What may be totally 'enchurched' in one context may be completely unchurched in another.

ENTERING ANOTHER'S TERRITORY

It is not surprising then, that contact between the unchurched and the pastor is so often marked by confusion and anger on both sides. But I do not want to imply that the desire to gain some control in a situation is by definition to be pastorally insensitive or dishonest. Especially when in distress, people often want someone from outside to take a measure of control. It is more a matter of *how* the control and definition the pastor gives to a situation helps or disables the family in managing a critical event.

The occasional offices of baptism, marriage and funerals – the usual context in which the pastor meets the unchurched – are all also rites of passage. All rites of passage involve a transition (or better still, in the case of the dead and dying, a *translation*) from one status of life to another which is by its very nature frightening. Lack of control coupled with the desire to bring a form of pattern or control to bear on the situation characterizes such moments. It is part of the function of religion to supply the means of control by providing a way of confronting the situation, containing the fears and anxieties presented by it, and mapping a possible passage through it. This accounts for the frequent experience one has, as a religious agent in these circumstances, of being invested, or even imbued, with a tremendous authority. It is crucially important to realize that this authority arises out of the human event itself and is therefore given to the minister *only for a time*. In these transitory moments the pastor can do work of lasting importance. If, on the other hand, we fail to recognize these moments for what they are – moments when people are potentially close to a sense of the sacred in life as it is given to them directly, not mediated to them by us; if we overvalue more structured and permanent patterns of contact with the unchurched, through courses of baptism preparation, or bereavement counselling and the like, we may actually prevent ourselves from doing effective work.

Taking the last point a bit further, pastors often have to decide whether they are willing to enter the family or household's territory, in which case they only remain there by invitation, or whether to insist that the people always come on to theirs. One can see that a strong motive in the development of marriage and baptism preparation classes, in the growth of the catechumenate movement, and the requirement that baptism should take place only in public liturgy, is the desire to control the environment in which matters of faith are raised. In this way pastors may extend the territory they may regard as their own. Again I am not saying that this is wrong, but that it should be openly acknowledged as a factor affecting pastoral contact. Very often people approaching marriage, or bringing a child for baptism, are unsure and apprehensive. They welcome the opportunity to have things discussed and explained, if only in order to know what is expected of them in the service. But it is still an invitation to come away from their own territory and on to one's own. This is not a problem as long as a pastor is aware that the element of control is present and is therefore sensitive to the feelings of defensiveness, resentment or fear it might evoke in some people. But if it is done without pastoral sensitivity, evading the issue of authority which is undoubtedly present, the pastor may feel they have done all they can, but a couple may go away feeling angry that something they felt was theirs and very precious has been hijacked by somebody else for their own purposes.

Perhaps it is the connotation of familiarity carried by the term 'folk religion' which is, after all, the main obstacle to a more real engagement with the cultural and religious diversity which characterizes the modern situation within and outside the churches. I have mentioned before how actual folk beliefs and practices were rediscovered in the nineteenth century by people whose desire for reform and mission led them to realize their own ignorance of what was actually the case. Today it may still be the missionary, rather than the pastor, who has a clearer understanding of how the Church is to engage with actual diversity. How Christian leaders choose to act in a particular situation depends very largely on how they define it. If they regard themselves as missionaries on foreign territory rather than pastors on their home ground, they will draw their boundaries very differently and not necessarily more exclusively. The missionary, used to working across cultures, understands much better than the pastor that it is an open question how far one should stand against prevailing elements of local culture and belief for the sake of the gospel, and how far, in order for the gospel to take root at all, it must be retranslated and handed over in an idiom which people can understand and own for themselves.

The missionary knows that nothing can be taken for granted, but that a common ground must be negotiated if the gospel is to be served in a particular situation. Vincent Donovan describes in his book *Christianity Rediscovered*[6] how, in order to reach the Masai in Kenya, he had to leave behind the home mission altogether and live among them, striving to translate the essence of the gospel in terms of their own struggles, rivalries and pattern of life, instead of bribing them with medicines and clothing to come to the home mission and instructing them there. In the process he came to realize how shallow the commitment to Christianity often was among those who were already assumed to be fully evangelized. The pastor, like the priests in the home mission in Donovan's Kenya, is much less likely than someone out 'in the field' to be aware of the critical distance which separates his or her own world of thought from those with whom he or she is occasionally in contact. In these circumstances they will often either assume too much or too little. But what causes offence among the unchurched is not a sense of distance or distinction between the organized Christianity of the pastor and their private beliefs, but the assumptions the pastor makes out of ignorance or insecurity. What unchurched people are asking of a pastor at the critical moments when they approach him or her for the occasional offices is not that the pastor should ignore differences but manage the transactions between them. But that requires from the pastor some real knowledge of *both* worlds, and imaginative sympathy for what may often seem strange and rather frightening.

The first step in successful pastoral contact with the unchurched is a frank understanding of the fluid and open character of modern society in which no one has absolute control over meanings and all of us operate different frames of reference according to the context. On a superficial level we know much more about each other than we ever did before, through what is reported via the media. On a more local and personal level we are even more ignorant than we were before, because the area of publicly accepted ritual and conventional ways of dealing with life-changing events like birth, marriage and death has shrunk so considerably. What frightens all of us most, pastors and unchurched alike, is our lack of control in situations which are often by their very nature situations of confusion, ignorance and fear. In this chapter we have looked at some of the factors which today make the level of confusion and pain even greater – the relocation of religion to the private sphere; the fragmentation of folk religion and its increasing separation from organized religion; the denominations' anxiety about their own role, status and degree of control over religious meanings. It is essential in such a situation that those committed to pastoral contact with the unchurched do it with a combination of caution, initiative, hopefulness and humility, aware of their own ignorance and preconceptions, and of the need to map the territory carefully, willing to see a human moment for what it is and to underline its importance, willing to act even when not in complete control of the context. Nobody is asking the pastor to avoid making definitions or offering interpretations to people which touch their own personal experience, least of all the unchurched. In some ways this is, religiously and pastorally speaking, the pastor's most important function. After all, rites of passage are all to do with leaving one defined state to enter another, which means drawing lines, establishing thresholds, determining what can be taken with you when you cross the line and what must be left behind. But we can only help this to be done properly by being critically aware of the forces involved, both open and submerged, and initially accepting the roles assigned to us as representatives of the Church or religion, however bizarre they may seem at first. Only then can we negotiate a space in which meaningful contact can be made and a real transaction take place. This often brings a measure of conversion on both sides.

Two models seem to me to be helpful in this context. The first is drawn from the account of Paul's visit to Athens in Acts 17. The whole situation in which much of the ministry to the unchurched takes place seems to require the same strategy that Paul adopts in this account. Paul takes a tour of the city of Athens. He knows it is full of idols, and their presence shocks him. But he cannot behave as he would if he were in Jerusalem. Athens is foreign territory. He has no privileged access to a hearing. In order to gain a hearing he must affirm what religion his hearers have, and use what religious symbols they possess to make his point. Nor can Paul control the way he is heard and how his hearers will react. A particularly familiar note is struck when he reaches what is for *him* the crucial point of his discourse, the resurrection, only to have his hearers say, 'We will hear you about this some other time.' Even Paul is forced to recognize when he hears this that the moment of encounter is over.

Similarly those of us involved in ministry to unchurched people must discover what is really there, and find ways of opening dialogue, using what we can of what is really there to begin it, affirming the religious feelings and beliefs which people already possess without losing our own integrity in the process – and at the end not feeling too disappointed when the 'window of opportunity' disappears again. Paul was not aware of the result of his efforts. Nor, usually, are we. His missionary strategy translates so well into our context because both are situations in which there can be no demand for a privileged hearing and very little or no control over the context in which the hearing takes place. The willingness to enter another's ground and to recognize it as theirs is the basic act of service demanded by the situation in either case. This act of service often brings us back into contact in the most profound way with the sources of Christian action and discipleship in the gospel.

The second model is drawn from the contemporary hospice movement in its care for the dying and their relatives. Christian faith undergirds the whole movement in the assertion of the importance of every human life even when all hope of continuing it has been lost, and of the right every person has to make a good death, which is an important *event*, not merely the cessation of life. The way this is expressed, though, is by sustaining the dying patients as much as possible to make their own choices, by attention to all their needs, physical and emotional as well as spiritual, thus creating the space in which healing may take place both for the dying individual and those close to him or her. Increasingly, it makes no difference in this process if the death takes place in the hospice itself or in a patient's or relative's home. It is the invitation extended by the patient and the patient's relatives to the team of professional carers, as well as vice versa, which creates the dimension of hospitality without which the hope of healing does not exist. Similarly, through the occasional offices, both parties are simultaneously hosts and guests in the other's world. Neither is totally in control. In these circumstances courtesy is not merely a social skill but a divine gift.

CONCLUSION

A T THE END of *The Clerical Profession*, Anthony Russell charts out three possible scenarios for the future of the Church and its ministry – the traditional, the adaptionist and the reformist. My sympathies are with the Church of the reformist future, which he describes in the following terms:

> [It] is essentially a movement in society rather than an institution . . . In its structure [it] is much more pluriform than the contemporary Church . . . A principal feature . . . is its low 'visibility' in society, for the Church sees itself as hidden within society as a popularist movement rather than set over against society in an institutional form.[1]

He goes on to describe the priesthood as the servant of the Church's ministry, and to speak of the necessity of having a focal person in each community who 'articulates, actualizes, "energizes" and epitomizes' the ministry and life of the local church. But he sees this role as one which has to be carried out humbly, entertaining the beliefs of others within and outside the congregation, listening and learning from others and making available to them his or her own faith, experience and pastoral skill.

That is the route I have tried to chart in this book, with the sources of its inspiration in the Bible, the tradition and contemporary life. The Church carries with it a lot of cultural baggage from the past, particularly associated with the role of the clergy. Whilst we cannot dispense with this baggage altogether without losing the ability to take our past into our future, the contemporary situation of cultural diversity requires us to travel light and to live as far as possible off the land. There is a great danger otherwise that we will become increasingly estranged in a cultural ghetto, sustained only by our own sense of exile, rather than reviving a sense of being on pilgrimage towards something new.

Pilgrimage is the great metaphor in a world in which so many are displaced and on the move without a sense of direction. In our society the 'sense of the holy' is itself something which has been displaced, banished from the centre of our lives and forced to exist on the fringes of our common experience as something powerful but inexplicable. Churches are sometimes as afraid as other professionally-led institutions of something which is beyond reason and often breaks through into common consciousness as the 'miraculous'. But if churches are to be places hospitable to the Spirit, they have to make room for a sense of the immanent presence of God as *'mysterium tremendum et fascinans'*. By very definition, this sense of the presence of God exists outside as well as inside the churches, and in our fragmented society it is often given expression in bizarre and antagonistic forms. Nevertheless, 'the wind bloweth where it listeth, and thou hearest the sound thereof, but canst not tell whence it cometh, and whither it goeth: so is every one that is born of the Spirit'. We have become too afraid, perhaps, of being like 'children, tossed to and fro, and carried about with every wind of doctrine' and not sufficiently aware of the opposite danger.

I remember, as a student, visiting the great church at Qal'at Siman in Syria, built as a place of pilgrimage around what remained of the pillar of St Simeon Stylites, one of the strangest Christian saints. As you look from the church itself on to the plain below you can also see the remains of the huge hostels which welcomed pilgrims to the shrine. We forget how close the association is between pilgrimage, travel and hospitality. 'A place of rest while on a journey' is a definition which covers all words like hostel, hotel, hospice, hospital. At centres of pilgrimage like Qal'at Siman they would have welcomed a huge variety of people from far and near. These motley individuals would have come to the shrine for all sorts of different reasons of their own, but also because the shrine itself was a symbol of what they sought – closeness to God.

Places of pilgrimage are as a rule more hospitable to the strange and the stranger than institutions entrenched in one particular community. Released from the usual barriers of class, race and custom, visitors may, in proximity to a shrine, find room for each other in a new sense of community. To provide a hostel for people on their way seems to me to be an appropriate goal for the pastoral ministry of the local church, because it takes more fully into account than some other models the fact that casual and temporary contact with people may be as important as more planned and permanent relationships; and that it is possible to offer an honest and effective ministry without being in control of the circumstances and context in which we work.

In their book on pilgrimage, the anthropologists Victor and Edith Turner describe cultural conditions in which new centres of pilgrimage have been established.[2] Very often they have been in circumstances of great tension, a sense of social disintegration and oppression of the spirit. Usually there has been a strong undertow of popular protest against these conditions, and a rediscovery of what the Turners term *'communitas'* – a spontaneous sense of community and individual identity arising out of the excitement of sharing a common vision.

Communitas is, as it were, at the opposite pole to the institutional life of the Church. It is potentially dangerous, irrational and intermittent, but arguably, unless the life of a church taps into it, its worship becomes dessicated and it loses the ability, as well as the will and intelligence, to touch the heart and imagination. The same anthropologists suggest that in modern society the Church is itself a sort of 'anti-structure' to the prevailing structures and norms of society. This implies that without the Church as the guardian of an alternative vision of community, society itself would be the poorer.

A less institutionally 'visible' Church might be better able to keep its modes of practice and activity in contact with the sources for making community which pop up in all sorts of unusual places, at pop concerts and weight-watchers, royal weddings and parish outings as well as in pastoral schemes and community work. Pastors as watchers and explorers, bridge-builders and guardians of communal memories and vision, sharing and reflecting back to the rest of the *laos* its own ministry, have a special role in keeping the Church in the way of pilgrimage and in touch with its own nature as a sacrament of God-given humanity in Christ.

NOTES

_____

INTRODUCTION

1 R. S. Thomas, 'The Priest', _Selected Poems 1946–1968_ (Hart-Davis, MacGibbon 1973).

1 MODELS FOR MINISTRY

1 In George Appleton (ed.), _The Oxford Book of Prayer_ (Oxford University Press 1985), p. 133.
2 Carlo Carretto, _The Desert in the City_ (Fount, 1979).

3 THE GOOD SHEPHERD

1 Jürgen Moltmann, _The Church in the Power of the Spirit_ (SCM 1977), pp. 128–9.
2 ibid., p. 129, my emphasis.
3 Sheila Cassidy, _Sharing the Darkness_ (Darton, Longman & Todd 1988), p. 71.

4 PASTORS AND PRIESTS

1 R. S. Thomas, op. cit.
2 Georges Bernanos, tr. Pamela Morris, _Diary of a Country Priest_ (Fontana 1963).
3 Urban T. Holmes, _Ministry and Imagination_ (Seabury Press 1976).

5 THE LURE OF PROFESSIONALISM

1 Quoted in Anthony Russell, _The Clerical Profession_ (SPCK 1984), p. 12.
2 ibid., p. 15.

6 'HOW SHALL WE SING THE LORD'S SONG IN A STRANGE LAND?'

1 Margaret Turk, ed., *Children in the Way* (Church House Publications 1988).
2 Church of England Board of Social Responsibility, *Church and Community Work* (1988), p. 6.
3 David Thomas, quoted ibid., p. 26.
4 Ann Morisy, article on Community Ministry published in *Laos*, Summer 1991 by the Lay Training Team of the Diocese of Southwark.

7 BODY LANGUAGE AND OTHER METAPHORS

1 Wesley Carr, *The Pastor as Theologian: Integration of Pastoral Ministry, Theology and Discipleship* (SPCK 1989), p. 67.

8 MEETING ON THE ROAD: PASTORAL CARE OF THE INDIVIDUAL

1 Victor Frankl, *Unconscious God*, quoted in R. F. Hurding, *Roots and Shoots* (Hodder 1986), p. 129.
2 See Eric Griffiths, 'Tenderness and Steadiness', *Times Literary Supplement* 7 June 1991, p. 13.
3 C. G. Jung, 'Psychotherapists or the Clergy' in *Psychology and Religion: West and East* (Routledge and Kegan Paul 1970), p. 339.
4 C. G. Jung, 'Psychoanalysis and the Cure of Souls', op. cit., pp. 350–1.
5 Robin Green, *Only Connect: Worship and Liturgy from the Perspective of Pastoral Care* (Darton, Longman & Todd 1987).
6 C. G. Jung, 'Psychotherapists or the Clergy', op. cit., p. 339.

9 PAINFUL ENCOUNTERS: PASTORAL CARE OF THE UNCHURCHED

1 Peter Berger, *The Sacred Canopy* was the American title of the book published in England as *The Social Reality of Religion* (Penguin 1973).
2 Thomas Luckmann, *The Invisible Religion* (Macmillan 1967).
3 David Hay, *Exploring Inner Space: Scientists and Religious Experience* (Mowbrays, revised edition 1987).
4 Keith Thomas, *Religion and the Decline of Magic* (Penguin 1973).
5 J. Obelkevitch, *Religion and Rural Society: South Lindsey 1825–75* (Oxford University Press 1976).
6 V. J. Donovan, *Christianity Rediscovered: An Epistle from the Masai* (SCM 1982).

CONCLUSION

1 Anthony Russell, op. cit., pp. 302–3.
2 V. and E. Turner, *Image and Pilgrimage in Christian Culture* (Basil Blackwell 1978).